The Exit Strategy

Michael Towers, MA

Copyright © 2018 Michael Towers

All rights reserved.

ISBN: 1985874768
ISBN-13: 978-1985874763

CONTENTS

	Preface	vi
	Prologue	ix
	Acknowledgement	xxxv
1	Introduction	Pg #1
2	Who Am I?	Pg #4
3	Interviewing	Pg #26
4	Time Management	Pg #42
5	Coaching	Pg #70
6	Progressive Discipline	Pg #95
7	Celebration	Pg #116

Preface

The Exit Strategy is the result of a management project that has been in development since the early 1990's. The concepts of The Exit Strategy have been tested in management groups and on supervisors with great success in many different businesses and organizational structures over the last couple of decades. The feedback has demonstrated that managers and supervisors have grown more confident in their roles and became stronger leaders along the way. The Exit Strategy has radically changed how they manage people and organizations have grown stronger after implementing The Exit Strategy.

The Exit Strategy begins by looking at three main descriptions, which are found in each of us, namely The Good, The Bad and The Ugly. The format of The Exit Strategy is built in such a way that it can be done in a series of group workshops or read through individually. This is a challenging and revealing book. It pulls today's manager away from the tendency to look at their employee as some sort of work machine and helps the manager look at the employee as an individual. If you can understand just a bit about your own presuppositions and methodologies that you bring to your management style and in turn how your employees relate to you then it is the belief and experience of the author that a much healthier work environment will be created.

The target market for The Exit Strategy is to those managers in the service industry with a largely seasonal base of employees. Such examples would be gas stations, quick-service stores, tourist destinations, hotels/motels, and other such-related places of business, although the concepts could be easily adapted for traditional places of business such as retail. The Exit Strategy has also been successfully utilized in non-profit organizations with staff larger than 20 employees that are community-based and delivering a number of client-centered services.

This is a confronting book, which quickly serves to make the person reading it uncomfortable. By probing beneath the surface and behind the motives of the manager, The Exit Strategy intends to help the manager understand the root and reason behind their actions and methodology. With the demands placed on the service industry today for high productivity and customer-focus it is important as a manager that you take your eyes off of the short-term results and focus on the bigger picture. You may be able to motivate people for the summer out of the use of fear tactics or outdated traditional management techniques from the 1980s and 90s but what damage is that doing over the long-term?

How are the things going on in your personal life effecting your management? What role does your background play into how you manage those around yourself? To what extent are your management decisions focused on meeting your own personal needs? Is this necessarily a bad thing? These are just some of the questions that The Exit Strategy addresses. It will truly change your life and the lives of your employees. This is a book that is meant to be studied and chewed on, all the while learning how to apply each principle to the workplace today.

With growing demands in the service industry from competitors and consumers alike the need to develop highly trained managers capable of handling all the pressures thrown at them is becoming increasingly more difficult. The service industry has the highest rate of manager burnout and the highest rate of employee turnover - both very expensive problems to the corporate entity trying to stay profitable.

In today's market where job satisfaction is quickly replacing money as the number one reason to stay in a job – The Exit Strategy is both timely and informative in helping create job satisfaction not only for the manager but also for the employees under that manager. If you are interested in generating long term positive results for you, your employees, and your business, perhaps this is a book for you.

The Exit Strategy can be thought of as being two sides of a coin. The Exit Strategy begins at recruitment and ends at termination. The graphic found at the beginning and the end of this book is the way you want your employees to look when they begin their job and also when they leave their job! Although I will talk about employee termination as a necessary aspect to employee management The Exit Strategy prefers to address termination as simply ***helping people leave***. It is the author's belief through experience that at least 80% of employees that have been terminated wanted to quit but couldn't for a variety of reasons. In other words, they preferred to be fired! The Exit Strategy turns that into a mutually beneficial experience for both the employee and the employer by emphasizing the idea that the employer is only helping the employee leave.

THE EXIT STRATEGY

Prologue

The phone on your nightstand begins to vibrate incessantly until it has worked itself up so much it falls to the floor below. Unscathed by your rejection it rocks you awake with a digital version of Bruno Mars' "The Lazy Song". Your arm emerges from beneath the covers and your hand blindly searches the nightstand before following the trail to the floor. Frustrated that someone would dare be texting you so early in the morning you grasp the phone and retract your arm to its hiding place beneath the blankets. The text reads, "gt a job. Luv Mom."

Subtle.

Although, truth be known, she has been hassling you for the last year to get out and get a job. You have made an effort but nothing has panned out. You just weren't meant to get a job yet. Or were you?

I know you don't fall for that line, "It's not you, it's me", but what if *it* was? I mean… What if the reason why you have not been called for an interview was because of you? Well, not really *you*, but that package in your hand that you are calling a resume? What *if* the only thing standing between you and your mom stopping texting you at that ungodly hour of 9am was those pieces of paper being crinkled in your hands as you walk into business after business? The Exit Strategy can help.

You see, this is a different sort of book. This is a book written by someone who has been a hiring manager for over the last 20 years. This is a book written by someone who has been forced to read and wade through thousands of pieces of paper just like yours. The agony of it all! Countless and countless resumes filling my desk in piles that ranges from horrible to bearable. Where do people looking for that first job learn how to write a resume? Why don't these people write a good resume?

It has been so bad that I have turned some interviews into a mini lecture on how to improve their resumes just because I was trying to make a difference one person at a time. No, they did not have what I was looking for, but they had *something* to offer. They just did not have a clue on how to capture it onto a piece of paper, which would get my counterpart down the street to look at their resume.

In an effort to be helpful I decided that I would write a book. My hope is that through my rants and stories on horrible resumes I have read over the years, you will be inspired to write that perfect resume; that resume which every manager dreams of receiving, to be framed and hung on their wall as an inspiration to all. They would then take every horrible resume and the person clutching it into their office and point to this magnificent resume, framed so elegantly and declare; "Now *that* is a resume!" they would beam as if it was their own child's accomplishment they were showing off.

I want to provide you with a humorous look at what to do and not do in preparing a resume. I used to believe that a person set out to create that perfect resume – that they were actually intentional on such a goal. They would go online and download some templates, replacing the nonsensical information with their relevant information and send it off. How unfortunate for them that they forgot to fill in all of the information, leaving some nonsensical information to be enjoyed by the manager at some later date. Or, they would turn to the family expert in helping them prepare their resume. This is helpful but just a heads up that you probably should check who you send the email to when thanking your mom for fixing your resume – especially if you are applying for a receptionist's position – just saying.

I guess I am concerned that the same care that these individuals have put into the preparation of their resumes has been lost today. Nowadays, resumes are full of spelling errors, incorrect punctuation, and poor grammar, text language so complex that Google can't even translate it or are simply incomplete. If I had a dollar for every time I have looked at a resume, was intrigued, and either went to email or call them for an interview, only to have the email come back and the phone message say out of service, well, I would have bought myself a really nice suit!

I am not going to teach you how to spell, how to punctuate, how to use correct grammar, or remind you to not use text language because chances are your hiring manager will not understand it. Go find someone else to show you those things. Instead, I will share with you what every employer thinks about resumes, longs to have in a resume, and most importantly if you want a job – what you should have in your resume!

So, the end result of your exhaustive effort in trying to get someone else – anyone really – to prepare your resume, is that most of the time it is a creative work of art that may be pleasing to the eye but holds no real value with a potential employer. In fact, I am surprised that I have not seen more copyright disclaimers or watermarks on the bottom of the resumes; Such as, "This resume was prepared by so-and-so" as a way of building their own portfolio. Sometimes, after meeting with the candidate I have been tempted to make the statement, "I'm not really interested in you as a candidate, however I would really like to meet the individual who prepared your resume…"

So often the employer will look at the pages of fanciful bold-faced foreign fonts filling them up, the colourful pages, the clear plastic covers, or the distinguished brown envelope, and place it in their file stuffed full of other fancy resumes in clear plastic covers or distinguished brown envelopes without even cracking the seal on the envelope.

So, *what* do employers look at when they look at a resume?

Well, before I attempt to examine that question I must first ask the more obvious question:

When do employers look at a resume?

I'm going to let you in on a little secret. Reading resumes is the least favourite part of a hiring manager's job. They do not want to read them. There is rarely anything enjoyable about reading them. So, thankfully a hiring manager has been designated to read these silly things only at specific times. And when is that specific time? That's right – only when they need to.

When the employer is hiring, the hiring manager will look at the most recent entries in the extreme resume makeover, opening up precious brown envelopes or squinting to read the type print on a bright neon background in the hopes that the first one or two will shine forth, thus ending this misery for another season. My hope is that once you have read this your resume will bring that breath of fresh air, like a spring bouquet of flowers, to the hiring manager. They would then stop once they have reached your resume, do a little jig around the office, and slide the rest of the resumes to its filing drawer located at the side of the desk.

Some of the hiring manager's frustration when looking at resumes today is the fact that they were never consulted by the 'experts' that are teaching the up and coming workers of tomorrow what is in and what is out in relation to constructing a good resume. The results are resumes piling up on employer's desks that are incomplete or formatted in such a way that they decrease the person's chances of *ever* getting that job.

Let us look at the source of this 'expert' advice on the construction of today's resumes. Oh sure, maybe an executive of a large corporation was given a phone call at one time, who in turn gave a polite and socially acceptable answer to the questioner, in order to gain some free advertising. No one ever stopped to question just how many resumes that executive may have looked at recently, or if he/she is drawing from their experiences in the mail room 25 years earlier!

Where can we go to get a more realistic perspective of what employers want in a resume? Well, it may not be the most glamorous of jobs, but collectively they represent the single biggest employer worldwide. Who are they? They are the chicken joint on the corner, the burger baron, the ice-cream hangout, the retail store in the local mall, and the gas station down the street. They are the fast food restaurant, the family restaurant, the Friday night 'place to be'. They are the coffee shop, the discount retail store, and the big box 'stuff-mart', and together they probably see more resumes in a given year then any corporation sees in its entire lifetime on Wall Street. The service industry is representative of the largest employer worldwide, and its managers can sift through hundreds of resumes at the beginning of each new season of business.

If you are looking for your first job then this is the place where you will likely find it, and so take it from someone who has spent 20 years as a manager in that industry, you need to hear what they have to say if you want to get that job! This book is a reflection of conversations I have had with my peers and other professionals in the same industry, hearing their frustrations with the quality of resumes they had to wade through, along with my own reflections coming from having read thousands of resumes during the course of my career.

So, since you're asking I will answer. When do they look at a resume? Well, you must first understand that if they are looking at resumes then they must be hiring. They would love to have the luxury of sitting in their offices one afternoon, looking at a handful of resumes thinking, "Oh, that one is good. I will place this resume in my special pile to interview in six months when I am hiring again."

It just does not work that way. If they are not hiring, they are not looking. And do they enjoy hiring? For the most part - no. Times have changed for both the employer and the employee. This means adjustments on both sides. In Canada, a growing trend amongst employees is a different type of motivation other than money. It would seem that young adults looking for work are not just looking for work but for a place to go to get money and have that schedule fit in with their social schedule.

Young adults are also looking for a different type of work environment, meaning they want to have fun while they work; they want to be given respect and feel like their voices are heard. If not, they will not hesitate in leaving their job and walking down the street to take another one. This trend results in the vast majority of today's young adult's resumes showing a work history of six months or less at any one place.

You need to appreciate how frustrating this may be for these managers, as they recall how difficult it may have been for them to get their job, and having it drilled into them since they were children, that even if you hated your job you needed to suck it up and deal with it because you should be thankful that you even have a job. You can imagine the distain some managers may have as they press their faces against the windows of their offices, looking out at those young adults whistling while they walk away from one job down to another one that will be a fun place to work. I wish I could say that even with the most recent unemployment situation in parts of Canada that some of that sage advice from our elders would be rubbing off on these young adults but it would appear not.

Even in places where it is difficult to find employment the young adults or first-timers to the whole job scene are bringing in these new attitudes. They want a fun place to work and they want to feel like what they have is worthy to be counted and employers are finally picking up on that. The result is that employers have made those changes and that lots of these first-job-service-orientated places have become a lot more appealing to work. So now that you find yourself actually wanting to work at some particular place, how in the world do you go about convincing that employer to hire you out of the hundreds of other potential candidates?

Hiring means taking time to look at these colorful, fluffy resumes - Sifting out the ones that really annoy them - Making some reference calls to individuals that don't want them working for them anymore, so they will go on about how great they were - Individuals that are in some way related to them and therefore will not want the backlash from the family over something said negatively - Individuals that barely remember who the person is, (They are always amusing to talk to: "and so Mr. Brown, what can you tell me about Joe?"

"Well I can hardly remember him but what I do remember is that he was an excellent worker, always on time and of course I would hire him again – (if I could only remember what he looked like!")

In my own practice, I have moved away from checking references. From an increase in Human Rights challenges and labour laws in favor of the employee, past employers are less and less hesitant in offering any sort of reference for an individual for fear that what they say can be used against them, especially if the applicant does not get the job.

I have also found that references do not tell us anything helpful about the applicant. The applicant, who may or may not understand the requirements of the job they are applying for, handpicked the references. Both ways, these references are in favor of the applicant getting the job, any job, and the expectation is that the references will say whatever needs to be said in order for the applicant to get the job. If you want to include references then in my experience the wow factor on the resume is that the applicant has gone out of their way to have a couple references write up letters to be included with the resume. Those will catch an employer's eye every time!

Then after checking the references comes the interviewing and more interviewing and then the reviewing of their resumes because they do not line up with what they are now looking at across the table from them.

(On a side note if you are ever in an interview and the employer keeps looking at your resume and then looks at you with a puzzled look on their face - it is pretty much over!)

Once the selection has been made comes the fun part - training. This, of course, is every employer's nightmare. You will find that in most cases the owner, the general manager, or whenever possible the shift manager, will try to find some excuse to not be around. There will either be a wedding for three weeks out of the country, lost vacation time from 5 years earlier, special conference on fly repellent held in some remote village in South America, or anything that will keep them away from the disaster that is sure to follow.

Here is a note on training. I have read several resumes where they demonstrate a high enthusiasm for the position, which possibly could simply be a desire to have a job – any job but they have no demonstrated skills applicable to the job listed. Training is costly, difficult, and yields short-term results for the service industry. Why? Because employers have come to understand that the vast majority of their workforce is seasonal or they are only there in the short-term. Therefore, the cost of fully training an employee into their position does not yield a good enough return since the probability of them leaving in six months is high.

Therefore, what employers are going to be looking for is some demonstrated level of competence or training found in a similar work setting, which will minimize any training that they would have to do with you and consequently will shoot your resume to the top of the pile. If you are looking for a position in which you will receive full and complete training, then don't look in the service industry. Go volunteer for an organization first or be prepared to have a few first job frustrating experiences until you can piece those failed attempts together in which you can now demonstrate that you have been 'trained' to your potential employer.

When do employers look at a resume? When they absolutely have to. With rising costs in training, lack of applicable skills taught in school today, and no job experience it will put the one with the resume in a tough position.

So here are some skills to learn when out with your glossy, photo-quality, neon pink resume looking for a job. I know that your lunch hour is probably a convenient time for you to go knocking on someone's door - but you need to realize that it is THE LUNCH HOUR!

This is true also for the supper hour, the late-night snack hour or pretty much any other hour that has more than one person in line to get something. And if you are looking to eliminate the embarrassment of going up to a restaurant during a busy time or to not bother someone if they are not hiring, so you phone first, here is what every manager would love to say to you but cannot because it would be impolite and against the human rights code, "No we are not hiring and can you please give me your name and number so I make sure never to hire you!"

You see, to an employer if there is not even the effort made to come up to their place of business and get ignored for the hour, while the customers are being served, then they do not want to put the effort into reading a resume nor talking to someone on the phone.

"Hello this is Jake. I was wondering if you are hiring right now?"

"Wow! Jake. This is just uncanny that you called right in the middle of my supper hour because I was just thinking about how I needed to hire one more person that was sensitive to all my customer needs. Let me walk away from this line up of customers and conduct an interview with you right now over the phone."

Okay, that will never happen!

So how do you know when a place is hiring? Well you do not, and that is the problem isn't it! My first real job I got by going up to the place every day at 3:15pm for one week. On the seventh day I walked in and I overheard the owner say "Oh man, it's that kid again. Just give him a job so he will stop annoying me!" For some reason I get really annoyed when individuals do that to me now, but you have to admire their tenacity!

There are the generally accepted times of year that most employers would want to hire or need to hire. These times would be April for the summer rush; August to supplement those going back to school and November for Christmas rush, if necessary. Employers generally expect to get a barrage of resumes at this time and schedule any necessary hiring around these times in order to lower their advertising costs in regards to hiring.

Now that we have determined when not to and when to drop off a resume; (I hope we are all clear that phoning is not going to increase your chances at getting a job!) let us look at what a resume should look like. Throw away all the pretty paper, the colorful backgrounds, the fancy envelopes, the perfumed pages and just focus on the substance.

Why throw that stuff away? Well, we are making assumptions that the employer will like the neon purple, scented, wild font type resume. Not every employer will appreciate the creative ability that you might possess. Best to keep a resume simple and plain.

Contrary to popular belief that somehow a bold color or fancy printing somehow hypnotizes the employer into reading that one resume out of the stack, just does not happen, and the people that sell you the colored paper and colored ideas trying to convince you that this is so are incorrect. I would wonder if these people would look at you and say;

"Yes, it was because I went with rouge 32 with a European bold font that I got this job!"

Save yourself a few dollars on paper and photocopying and put substance and not fluff into your resume.

Why is your name always the boldest item on your page? It is interesting with those resumes that come across my desk with their names, addresses, and ten phone numbers to contact them, which take up half the page because of their size. Bigger is not always better on a resume.

"Oh, well, look at that. Mary's name is so big that it needed four pages to put it on. That tells me that Mary is quite the worker."

Not quite how it works. For the most part the employer looking at a good resume will go, "Wow! This is a good resume - now whose is it?"

In other words, the employer will look for the name as the last thing. Yes, still keep your name at the top, maybe eliminating five or six contact numbers, and you can make it smaller and not so 'in your face' as before.

Let us spend some time looking at your job experience section. I know that you may have had a lot of job experience such as Joe's mill from August '16 to Sept '16 and at Mary's car wash from June '17 to June '17, but is there any value putting them on your resume?

As a general rule do not put any job experience down on your resume unless you have worked there for a minimum of six months. Why six months? As a perspective employer, we want to know that you will be with us for one season of business! As mentioned earlier the trend today is for these shorter periods of employment. Keeping in mind the picture of the manager pressing their face against the window in envy as you walk away to a 'better place to work' down the street, you need to ask yourself the question; Why do you want to list a shorter work experience on your resume?

What skill did you learn from working at Mary's car was for a month in '17? What message do you want to communicate to this potential employer? Are you just rubbing it in that you have the luxury to walk away from a bad work environment? Or are you communicating that you lack the skills necessary in keeping a job? Both are negative messages to the employer so make sure you are clear as to why you want that on your resume. Try to explain that at Mary's car wash you learned how to make deposits and balance the till each day, however the work schedule interfered with the sports team you were on and that is why you are looking for other employment. Something like this goes a long way in neutralizing the stinging effects of a short-term work experience on a resume.

The problem with short-termers on a resume is that they can communicate many different inaccurate messages. You need to be clear on your resume for your reasons on leaving if you are including jobs that you have been at for six months or less. You may have had legitimate reasons for leaving, such as not enough hours even though your availability was Tuesday night from 4pm to 5:30pm and Saturday morning before 10am, or that you found a better paying job leaving your last job making 11.45$/hour to now making 11.35$/hour?! (Make sure you check your math if you do indeed put such things on your resume) These reasons may be valid for you but will they make sense to the potential employer?

Or better yet you may have been laid off. I like that one. Laid off. I look at a resume that the person started in June of one year working until July of the same year only to "unexpectedly" get laid off. How unfortunate for them to get laid off right in the middle of the busiest time of the year. Now mind you not everyone would purposely lie on their resume but there are more creative ways of doing that then this.

Now that I have brought up the issue of lying on their resume I should address it. From an employer's perspective it is relatively easy to identify a resume in which there have been some, um, creative embellishment on the content. It is the same reason why mothers are able to convince their children that they have eyes on the backs of their heads or why dads can give you that look like they are not a brick short of a full load as you had once hoped. It is our experiences that give us the leg up on identifying those suspect resumes, and there's a lot of them floating around out there.

Not only may we have done the very same thing when we were starting out but like I mentioned earlier I have read literally thousands of resumes, personally hired well over a thousand people during my career and probably fired just as many. That accumulated experience gives the manager a certain level of 'street smarts' in which the con job you are trying to pull on the employer was just tried by the previous dozen applicants. We are wise to you so don't try to pull the wool over our eyes any longer. The market is too competitive for you to get away with it for any extended period of time.

The next point about job experience that I want to mention is that you should only list those jobs that have even the slightest resemblance to what you are currently applying for. Listing a bunch of jobs working in the forest, on the beach, cutting wood, sorting wood, cleaning picnic sites etc., and then applying for an office position just does not go together.

Chances are the perspective employer would pick up on the fact that you would spend most of your time staring out of a make shift window that you drew on your cubicle wall, dreaming about everywhere but where you are.

Be honest here. If you do not have related job experience then do not list anything. You need to be able to demonstrate how your previous job experience is going to help you in the job that you are applying for now. It is not like a video game where you accumulate experience points for completing 'tasks' and that will somehow get you into this new 'level'. You need to have a reason for putting it on your resume and if you cannot find a way of connecting all those forest-situated jobs to the cubicle-situated job then you are best to not include any of it on your resume.

If your jobs consisted of a weekend here and there over a two-month period then do not list that as well. The fall back to this is if the employer picks up from your resume that you are a young student, maybe in grade 10, and you have limited job experience, that is to be expected and could work to your benefit, but if you are 26 and have the same amount of job experience as the grade 10 you have a problem.

To combat this shortcoming, you could use a great fallback tool; volunteer work. You see, you need to have something on that resume besides hanging out playing pool with the guys that indicates that you were responsible for something, over some period of time, working with somebody.

If it so happens that you did this on a volunteer basis then all the better since what you will end up making will be pretty much equivalent to a volunteer's salary anyway. So, put it down. Volunteer work also needs to be consistent with what you are applying for.

Take a hard look at your resume and ask yourself this question. If your previous work experience does not line up with what you are applying for, or if your volunteer experience does not line up with what you are applying for, then why are you applying for it? If your answer is 'cause it is a job, then the chances are you will not get that job. Employers need people who want to be doing what they are paying people to do. They cannot afford to give somebody a job 'cause it's a job. Competition is too stiff and jobs to scarce to have the luxury to hire someone who will spend their time looking for the next big break.

This point continues to amaze me. Every time I post a position I can expect an immediate 25% of the applicants to be applying just because it is a job. This isn't necessarily a bad thing but when they communicate that message to the potential employer it does not do well in having their resume make it out of the filing cabinet to the side of the desk. If you don't put in the effort to convince the employer that you really want this job for something other than the fact that it is one then please do not expect the employer to take any amount of time to even look at your resume. It just is not going to happen.

So, what else should you include on your resume? A popular section but one that I have yet to understand is hobbies or sports. Here is some advice about this section. Unless you are applying for a computer programmer with EA Games or something where "lifestyle" is a prerequisite for the job, I would suggest ever so politely, not to include anything about this on your resume. How exactly would it help in your chances to get a job if you listed off that you enjoyed baseball, skiing, hunting, fishing, motor cross, hand gliding, bungee jumping and the list goes on. This is what the employer sees when they look at that section. This person is unavailable for this time, that time, and no time. Why should I hire them?

You probably thinking that you are flexible in your schedule and that you are willing to work around your hobbies. But your hopeful employer does not know that, and you certainly don't want to add a disclaimer under this section stating so. That just will not work in convincing the perspective employer so best just to remove this section all together.

Accomplishments are always a good thing to add but only under two conditions. One is that your accomplishments are fresh and new. In other words, do not put down on your resume that in grade 6 you received an award for perfect attendance, since that does not tell us anything about how your attendance is right now. In fact, as an employer I would be looking at that and be asking myself, "Why hasn't this person won the award since then?"

Something like that can only damage your chances at an interview. The second condition is that the awards or accomplishments are relative to the job you are applying for. A certificate of appreciation for all of your hard work with the local food bank, as an example, is relative to applying for a job in the service industry because of the constant interaction that you would have with people, along with a variety of other skills learnt in that environment. An honour roll award is also applicable as it demonstrates several good qualities to a perspective employer.

How long should this resume be?

May I suggest that if you need to buy more paper in order to finish your resume we have a problem. The maximum that any resume should be is two pages for any entry level position. This is not based on any study or any master's degree in business or human psychology but simply on real life. The attention span of a perspective employer who will be the one who reads those resumes is the equivalent of two pages worth of information. Anything longer and it interferes with all the other crisis's arising, or the phone ringing, or the customers asking questions, or pretty much anything else that would come into their typical day. Once again, shorter is always better.

Certificates are nice, but please make sure that if you are going to ask this employer to muster the strength, stamina, and time to look beyond the two pages you have already supplied them with, then make sure it is worth it to them. A certificate in dog grooming if you are applying for a restaurant job just doesn't cut it. A certificate for serving it right if this business serves no alcohol is not really applicable either.

The other factor with certificates is to note the date on them. If you are thinking that your chances are improved if you had Food Safe and you're applying for a job in the food industry, but the date on your certificate is five years old, then chances are the employer will notice that as well. A couple questions during the interview about food safe practices will clearly illustrate to the employer just how well you remember some course that you 'needed' to take for a class several years earlier.

So, once you are done this process and you have put away your scissors and your glue then take a look at the finished piece. A plain, two-page, to the point, informative resume with maybe your accomplishments listed in a bolder text and your name taking up only a couple of lines. Do you feel good about what you have? Is everything written down true and complete? Have you managed to get rid of all the fluff?

If your answer is yes, then fight that urge to spray it with perfume and sprinkle sparkles all over it and go make some copies!

Don't place it into a brown envelope or even a bright red one. Get on some good clothes, wash your hair, comb your hair, take out your best pair of sneakers, and hit the pavement.

Now as you wait patiently off to the side for an hour, only to be instructed to give your resume to the cashier, you can hand it over with confidence, knowing that up to this point you have done everything possible to increase your chances of getting a job. You have designed a resume that every employer wants to read. You have given them what they want. Good job!

Now go get ready for that interview!

So, You Got An Interview!

THE EXIT STRATEGY

Out of the dozens of resumes that your perspective employer looked at they decided to give you an interview. Great! Obviously, my hints and tips that you followed above helped! (Or, you did the complete opposite and that worked - whatever - what is important is that you got that interview - right!?).

So, what do you do now that you have to go to an interview in which the entire thing will be decided in the first thirty seconds?

Did I just say that in the first thirty seconds the interview will be decided? Yes.

For most employers they have determined whether you are right for the job based on your resume. Now it is a test to see if you are in fact the same person you wrote about. This takes us back to what I said before, in which I encouraged you to make sure that your resume is true and accurate. Although the employer may not say anything to you during the interview, you can know that if you show up and demonstrate the absolute opposite to what your resume says, they will wait patiently for the opportunity to end the interview. Their mind will already be made up.

Let me share with you a true story. Almost twenty years ago, I underwent a major career change. I had spent seven years with this particular company. My career had come to a standstill. I decided that I would follow my own advice in the first part of this book and write my own resume.

I kept it simple, one and one-half pages long with no interests listed. It listed my job experience, outside accomplishments in the last four years, and my internal awards that I had received in the last four years. I summarized what I felt were key skills that I had, which might be viewed as an asset to a potential employer. These skills were my extensive communication training, crisis line training, facilitation and mediation skills. (I know, it is amazing what one would find as an asset in management!) I then did some research and carefully applied for those jobs that I felt that I might do well in and enjoy.

Finding something that I might do well in and enjoy limited my choices considerably, and I ended up applying for only a small handful of jobs out of the hundreds that I looked at. Then I got the call. It was within a couple days of sending in my resume that they called me to set up an interview.

The first interview was to be over the telephone. I took advantage of this time before the call to research everything I could about this business. The phone call would take place in a few days so I had lots of time to make sure I clearly understood the philosophy and culture as much as possible of this business. When the phone call came we ended up talking for two hours. I felt very good about that interview and those feelings were confirmed. I had indeed passed the first interview and will now meet with their boss in person to have the second interview. This second interview happened almost one month later and in a neighboring city.

Now during this month I found myself working constantly without any days off, and near the end of the month I was working double shifts. At this point the interview was only three days away but I had already worked 20 days in a row. This particular week I would be opening the store and then closing the store every day. On the day of the interview I opened the restaurant, went home and quickly changed, drove to the neighboring city and had the interview, drove back home, changed and went back up to work to close the restaurant.

To make matters worse, I had hurt my back earlier in the week, and so sitting for long periods of time would aggravate the situation, causing me to squirm in discomfort every few moments.

So, after popping some heavy-duty pain medication I got into my vehicle and drove to the interview.

I arrived a half hour early. The time dragged as I waited for the interview to start. I paced up and down the store and looked in every corner trying to waste the time away. No doubt about it I was nervous. I was also on pain medication and tired and thinking about my store.

In other words, I was not there mentally nor was I prepared for this interview. Then the interview started. Amazingly their questions were exactly the same as the telephone interview. This should be a snap I thought to myself but that was not to be. Only after about 45 minutes it was apparent that the pain medication was not lasting, and I was squirming in my seat to offset the shooting pain up my back.

For reasons I can only blame on my lack of sleep and back pain I decided to answer all of these questions in a completely different way than I had originally over the phone.

For the two hours that I sat there squirming in that chair, in that office, I told the interviewer each of my failures; Where I had gone wrong as a manager, where I had fallen short of expectations, where I had lost respect of my employees and the list goes on.

Perhaps I justified it to myself at the time that this person would appreciate my complete honesty, or perhaps I was so completely tired and drained from all that was going on, but whatever the reason I never stopped.

Near the end of the interview I started sharing some of my "grievances" that I had with my head office, for they had just messed up again in my store, and I was irritated with their incompetence.

I decided (for I suppose temporary insanity had set in) to share in detail these 'frustrations' with this person sitting in front of me interviewing me for a perspective career.

It turned out that the person interviewing me was the Vice President of Relations for this company that I wanted to work for! Funny thing I knew this bit of information two hours prior when this whole nightmare began but it never stopped me!

The interview was over and I arose from my chair with pain shooting up my spine and shaking her hand I left the room. Walking out into the parking lot I knew right away that I had just done absolutely everything that I would instruct someone NOT to do for an interview.

I knew that I did not get the job and that was confirmed three weeks later with a polite phone call and a follow-up letter telling me that they were looking for someone "more qualified".

So, what can we learn from my painful experience? Well, we can glean several points from what went wrong in order to know what to do for an interview.

1. Get enough rest. Believe it or not an interview can take a lot of energy to get through. Being as well rested and relaxed as possible can help toward "keeping you fresh throughout the interview".

2. Do not book other appointments or obligations just before or after an interview. Such things serve as a distraction to you that can easily be picked up from the person conducting the interview and can be interpreted as not caring or lack of focus.

3. Do not go to an interview in pain. If you have hurt yourself or are in pain for some reason, either let the interviewer know prior and try to reschedule for another day or let them know right at the beginning of the interview so they will filter your body movements through that piece of information.

In my case the person interviewing me had no knowledge that I had hurt my back but observed me for two hours squirming on my seat and arching my back. To them I either needed to go the bathroom really bad or felt uncomfortable being there. Both would be seen as a 'negative thing'.

4. Keep your answers consistent. If this is a second interview, or if the interviewer is repeating their questions, make sure that you give the same answer each and every time. If you wish to elaborate on your answer, which is what the interviewer is looking for you to do, keep the elaboration simple and short.

5. Do not be negative. Yes, honesty is looked for, and to a certain degree talking about a particular time that you fell short of expectations may lean in your favour, but here is the bottom line in this area; This employer will spend only a few minutes with you, and in that very brief period of time, needs to see if you will be a good fit for what they are looking for.

You are selling yourself here so sell! A used car salesman does not draw the attention of the perspective buyer to the dent in the rear quarter panel, but instead to the CD player or the chrome wheels. Sell yourself by focusing on your accomplishments and what you can bring to the job, because the reality is that the employer is smart enough to know that there will be qualities about you that fall short of their expectations, but they need to know if the good will outweigh the bad!

I did apply for a different job shortly after receiving this rejection letter and after following all my advice just mentioned I ended up being offered a position with the company!

The job market is changing out there and employers are adjusting to the ever-changing demands of business and customers. This means that they are ever-changing in their approach to hiring and what they look for in potential employees. What might have worked to get you that job delivering pizzas three years ago will more than likely not work in getting you the serving job today.

Understanding the job before you apply for it is a step in the right direction. If you can grasp just a bit of the philosophy and/or culture of a company prior to going through the interview process, you will find that this bit of knowledge can help 'carry' you through the interview very successfully. Nowadays a quick read through the company's webpage or social media presence will provide more than enough information to help prep you for the meeting.

General skills that are generally looked upon favorably by most employers today would be: Communication, problem-solving, people interaction and customer service (not necessarily in that order). Rising costs of training, wages, and insurance makes hiring people without these skills unprofitable to an employer.

Therefore, it is important that you do what you can do to gain these skills. Let us talk about these skills in just a bit more detail. In today's highly competitive market it will be these skills that set you apart from that other person who was just going in for their interview.

Good communication skills do not mean that you are that person who will never shut up!

Communication surprisingly has more to do with listening then it does with talking. It means learning how to communicate positive messages through your body language. It means to convey a message to the person you are communicating with that they are special and worth your time and complete attention.

Not focusing on the talker, or folding your arms, or hunching over, all can communicate a disinterest in what the person is saying. Maintaining eye contact, keeping your arms away from your face and having your body positioned right in front of the person speaking, will all communicate your desire to hear what they are saying.

Using something called empathic listening also communicates worth and value to the individual you are speaking with. Empathic listening is like reflective listening where you would comment on what the person is saying such as "It sounds like that volunteer experience was very challenging for you." This would give the listener a chance to agree with you, letting you know if you are listening correctly, or to correct you and help you better understand what it is they are saying. It takes time to develop this skill so take advantage of every opportunity you can and solicit feedback from your family and friends as to how good a communicator they think you are!

Problem-solving could easily be lumped in with other skills like time management and organizational skills. They go hand in hand with decision making abilities and analytical skills. All really have to do with the same thing:

Can you follow procedures and policies on your own and learn to think for yourself in an efficient way?

Surprisingly this skill is often lacking in an entry level candidate, which typically is the high school/college student, or to put it another way - yourself! You would think that this skill would be more defined in this age group considering they spend all their time in school learning such things as this. So why is this not so?

Well in my observations, working for so long with this segment of the working group, I have noticed that if directions and step by step processes are explained, and/or listed for this person, they will perform and complete them far better than any other working group.

The difference comes when this person is now working on their own and is left to perform these same functions. Unfortunately, it seems that in this scenario the person has difficulty taking in all that is happening around them and is not able to make quick decisions.

An example would be a student working at a hamburger shop whose job is to get the buns ready for the burgers. When shown and supervised this student performs the job very well and very efficient. When left alone (not supervised) there is a tendency for the student to perform under expectations. Why is this so?

My theory is that the opportunity within school for a student to learn in a structured way has been overshadowed with the push to focus on their creative thought processes. What happens therefore is we end up with very independent workers which have no idea how to effectively follow procedures and/or policies. From an employer's perspective, this type of employee seems flighty, unfocused, easily distracted, and 'in their own world'.

This skill is generally a difficult one to teach and is best learnt through experience. I have found that those with strong procedure/policy skills are those individuals that have a lot of volunteer experience.

It seems that exposure to different structured situations outside of the school environment, helps tremendously in the learning of these particular skills. My suggestion to you, if you find you are weak in these areas, is to spend some time volunteering for any community group. Not only would that look good on your resume but it will help in your personal development as well!

When people-interaction is talked about it seems to exclude those that are normally shy, or reserved, or 'introverted' in nature. That is not the case though. People interaction is more about respect of the individual then it is about how you interact with someone.

Lack of respect is probably the leading cause of 'racist attitudes' toward individuals that we deem 'different' then ourselves. Those individuals that have a healthy respect for their elders, their parents, and their leaders, tend to carry that skill over into the business world, where the elderly, handicapped, or people of a different race would more commonly be.

THE EXIT STRATEGY

I remain astounded that we are still running into people that lack the respect which they should have for all peoples around them. This can make or break a business and therefore employers take this skill very seriously. For you - the potential employee - you will actually represent the business to the customer. In other words, you are the company. You can make or break this business just in the attitude that you carry over to each person you serve.

It is a serious responsibility and one that the employer does not take lightly. Even when you go into your interview how you act toward the customers that are there, other employees working, or the interviewer will be closely watched by the employer. Make sure that as you shout to the world demanding respect that you give it out as well.

Now in some ways customer service is tied into people interaction but leans toward ability more than respect. Customer service is all about making sure the customer is completely satisfied before leaving the place of business. Because the reality is if the customer is not completely satisfied, the chances of them coming back are not very good.

What are some universal skills in customer service that you can focus on right now, in order to set yourself up for success in this area?

1. Knowledge of the products and/or services
2. Learn to anticipate the customer's needs
3. Interact with the customer with enthusiasm
4. Make the effort to go beyond the customer's expectations
5. Focus on cleanliness before and after customers have been served
6. Thank the customer for coming and invite them back again
7. Interact with other employees in a professional manner always
8. Spend time making sure that all of the customer's questions and concerns have been answered to the customer's

satisfaction
9. Provide accuracy in all that you do for the customer
10. Have fun!

Once you learn these ten items and put them into action you will have mastered the skill of customer service and will have created an appeal about you for that potential employer.

All these skills are obtainable without having to get a job. Through groups that you are involved in or volunteer work that you do, these skills will be and can be learned, and I would encourage you to seek out those opportunities. Then during the interview, it will give you all the opportunity to talk about these great skills that you can bring to the workplace. You're the one! You have what it takes!

Congratulations! You have the job!

Acknowledgement

Everything I discovered about the psychology of management I learned from dead chickens. No serious. I spent years working for Kentucky Fried Chicken as a general manager and after engaging in debate after debate about the difference between a back and a thigh (just look in a mirror!) I came to an important conclusion. Perception is everything! When you hear excuses from the customers that they are allergic to the dark meat of a chicken and therefore can only eat white meat you realize that if someone believes something that somehow makes it true. Such is the case with psychology. The key to psychology is to get you attached to some title or condition or something that you can really sink your teeth into and believe.

Studying human behavior proved to be a very rewarding exercise during those years - especially when the customer became upset. Now it is not that I would purposely make the customers upset (most of the time anyway!) but when it did happen it proved to be a great opportunity to see a person "act out". Psychologists love talking about this and observing this so allow me to explain my theory of what "acting out" is. When a customer enters into the restaurant they are walking in with a pile of luggage with them. We can't see this luggage but that doesn't mean it isn't there right? That reminds me of a quick little tidbit I once heard which went something like this: Do you see an invisible elephant in the piano? No? Then that means that there is an invisible elephant in the piano. Anyway, where was I? Oh yes, the invisible luggage.

So, this customer drags this luggage up to the counter and orders a bucket of chicken. The cashier proceeds to explain to this customer that there is a 20-minute wait for chicken. At this moment an important thought process has occurred within the mind of this particular customer. Just like Mr. Dressup and his tickle trunk this person carries around a special piece of luggage. In this bag is every time they have been fouled out in a ball game or sent to a corner by a teacher or been cut off by a crazy motorist. In the millisecond that follows a decision is made as to what costume the customer wants to put on. Will it be the crazy mad man costume or the militant commando laying siege to a critical hill? Or perhaps the loud and obnoxious bum or the clown? The possibilities are endless. As they put on their costume they begin to "act out" whatever play of their life that they have decided to do.

To the cashier this could take on many forms but most of them negative. Now because the cashier is an employee being paid to stand there and tell the customers that there is no chicken they aren't allowed the freedom to reach into their "tickle trunk" or else it would add the much-needed balance to this one-sided play. After accomplishing all that the customer wants to do they quickly put their costume back in their bag for next time. They have completed their "acting out". To the casual observer though we wouldn't notice all that just went on. We would simply look at each other and say "It is just chicken! It isn't like the world just ended or something!"

Now the funny thing about what just happened above was that all this took place in public. You would think that most acting out would be done in private where one would feel secure and safe enough to act like a fool. Alas! The opposite is true! Acting out in front of complete strangers who for the most part you would probably never see again becomes much safer for most people. These people are doing what they always wanted to do around the dinner table but didn't because they just knew that their significant other would just raise their eyes and without missing a beat tell them to get a life or something non-validating like that! Family always has a way of doing that.

This book is a result of almost thirty years of observing people acting out in public places. Enjoy.

Introduction

Welcome to management! To get to this point you would have successfully made it through the first three months of your probation period, filled with excitement, stress, and many difference challenges. The focus shifts now from helping you do your day to day job to helping you learn how to manage the people on your team. I want to invest in you. I am not interested in just helping you be a great manager, I want you to be a great leader. There is a difference and to get there will require a lot of work and determination. However, you are surrounded by many people committed to seeing you succeed. Let's begin!

To help you succeed I am using The Exit Strategy. The Exit Strategy is a management methodology that I originally developed in the mid to late 1990s back when I was working for corporate in the restaurant industry. I found that this strategy helped develop future leaders, it led to reductions in staff turnover and it increased employee loyalty. When the Exit Strategy was first introduced it was a revolutionary way of approaching Human Resources, contrary to the old power-orientated management strategies of the 1980s and 1990s. Now, however, as Human Resources have changed and adapted over the decades, this philosophical approach to high-level employee engagement has become more of the norm. What keeps The Exit Strategy fresh and effective is its innovative way of looking at managing people that begins at recruitment and ends at termination.

You are a manager today because somewhere along your career path someone believed in you and thought that you were 'management material'. You had people work hard to develop you, equip you, and prepare you for this whole new world of management. In particular the management of people. However, now that you are in management, you may have noticed that the management of people is not as easy as these individuals may have led you to believe. In fact, you may have noticed that once you were in management they threw their keys on your desk and ran away giggling.

Perhaps the hardest part of managing people is that as you stare out at your team you realize that you have all of these sets of eyes staring back at you. They are looking to you for direction, for inspiration, for instruction, and for an example. It is hard for you to have an 'off-day' without someone noticing or to make a mistake without some employee bringing it up at some later date. The hardest part of all is realizing that your employees – sometimes – just aren't that into you.

A study by Dale Carnegie and MSW Research[i] polled a national representative sample of 1,500 employees across a wide range of industries and found only 29% of respondents to be fully engaged. Disengaged employees clocked in at 26% and a majority of workers fell somewhere in-between (i.e. putting in the minimal amount of effort to achieve expected results.) That means nearly half of employees aren't really into their jobs. This adds up to literally billions in losses--the Bureau of National Affairs estimates that U.S. businesses lose $11 billion annually due to employee turnover.

The study found engagement is most effected by an employee's relationship with his or her immediate supervisor. This is good news; management style is, after all, something that can be changed. To drive employee engagement, we need managers who communicate well and are able to create a culture of growth, recognition and trust. In other words, successful management isn't about personality; it's about results. It doesn't matter if managers are introverted or extroverted, timid or bold, loud or quiet, as long as they are making people feel like they are growing, appreciated, and confident in their future in our organization.

Before you read any further you will need a piece of paper and a pen.

THE EXIT STRATEGY

Personal Exercise: Build a house.

Take a blank piece of paper and turn it on its side. Draw a line along the entire bottom of the page. Go up about two inches on your page, on either side, and connect the sides by drawing a connecting line. You should now have a long rectangle at the bottom of your piece of paper. This is the foundation of your house.

Next, draw the walls and the roof of your house. You can draw a couple of windows and a door if you would like.

Looking back at your foundation I would like you to divide it into five sections. Take a couple of minutes, write down the five most important people in your life, and write their names down in each of the five spaces. Then I want you to write a reason or two as to why they are so important to you.

If you are doing this as part of a workshop then have a couple volunteers share a name or two from their foundation. Get them to list the name and the reason.

Get the participants to look at their foundations and then tell them that their third name is now gone, removed from their foundation. Get some feedback from the participants as to how they now feel, knowing that this person is now removed from their foundation.

The initial emotional reaction around the loss of this person from your foundation is quite normal and is a reaction to the very real need that they were providing for you. Take some time to reflect on your relationship with this person and try to articulate what the need was that they provided for you.

Who Am I?

I was still very much a teenager, albeit an older teenager, when I was co-managing a very busy family restaurant in the lower mainland of British Columbia, Canada. On one particular busy weekend when the restaurant was completely full an older career waitress had enough of my cocky attitude and decided to let me know what she thought. Holding a full coffee pot in one hand and gesturing wildly with her other hand she stood in the middle of the lobby area of the restaurant and proceeded to tell me off. It was one of those instrumental and life-changing moments that stays with you – all of the sights, sounds, and smells of the moment. Even now, as I recall the moment, I shudder.

What came out of that event changed my management approach, although to be honest the full transformation would take another few years while my pride and cocky attitude worked itself out of me. I had lost respect from my staff and back in those days that took an awful lot of work to do considering position brought about unearned respect all day long. The head cook would mock me – declaring that I wasn't skilled enough to butter toast. Even the dish pit guy looked down on me! I worked hard to try and earn the respect of the staff in that restaurant but being the youngest employee there didn't help and, in the end, when I finally moved on I had only been successful with a select few.

The Exit Strategy is very much a trial and error evolution of a successful management system. I was fortunate that throughout my management career I had been called upon to do the training and development so I always had an audience to try out different methods and different approaches. Then, when I worked for corporate I was able to expand my training and development – reaching a far greater pool of employees to experiment with in regards to the Exit Strategy methodologies. Over the last two decades I have refined this work in each organisation I was a part of and now as I come to the end of my career in training and development I wanted to finally put The Exit Strategy into print.

Let's begin unpacking the Exit Strategy by looking in a mirror. After all, this is what your staff and those who will be following your leadership will see. And who do they see? Who are you? The more you can understand who you are the better equipped you will be as a leader. This is your primary form of self-care; that act of understanding who you are. Therefore, self-care means understanding who you are and if you start there then you need to start with the question, "Who am I?"

An important first step in your personal development is the ability to objectively identify your strengths and your weaknesses. Striving to be someone you are not will always lead to bitter disappointments and personal failures, resulting in feelings of inadequacy and guilt. To hold up a mirror to yourself may be one of the hardest tasks that you do. It will give you little comfort to realize that as you begin to see your weaknesses and your flaws, those around you have already seen them for quite some time.

Through this section, I will start unraveling yourself to reveal the Good, the Bad, and the Ugly. The more honest you are will determine how successful you will be in answering the question; "Who am I?" I will look at your strengths, your weaknesses, and your dark side. I will also look at several aspects of who you are; what you believe, what is your culture, your morals, your personal standards, your long-range goals (both personal and business), your expectations, your hurts and pains, and your successes. These all play an important role in helping you answer that question; "Who am I?"

The Good

For some people this is going to be more difficult than looking at the Bad. Generally, people become shy or embarrassed when asked to identify their strengths. Only when an individual becomes confident in their ability to perform a strength, will they freely mention it in describing themselves. Others have absolutely no problem in rattling off endless lists of their perceived strengths only to realize later that they were only fooling themselves. You need to start with an inventory. Take a few moments right now to compete a list of individuals, groups, places, or times, which make you feel secure and protected. Give as much detail as possible. Be as honest as possible. Think of a best friend and a quality about them that appeals to you. Think about a club or organizations that you belong to that you feel good about. Why? What is it about that place, or that person, that makes you happy?

Name of person, group, place or time	What is the quality that makes you happy?

What you have done is to create a list of your needs. These are important to recognize in understanding who you are. If any of these people, clubs, or times, were to disappear, you would subconsciously find yourself searching to find a suitable replacement. As an example, if you listed your best friend Bob because he always knows the right thing to say to comfort you, but now Bob is gone, you might find yourself trying to make your other friends into Bob. You would never be able to replace Bob, but your underlining need that you received from Bob was comfort. Recognize that another friend of yours may be trying to show you comfort but in his/her own special way. This is a step in the right direction to fulfill that need without projecting unrealistic expectations upon any individual.

Now take some time to complete the following personal inventory. Answer as completely as possible the questions giving as much detail as you can. What you are doing in this exercise is determining your limits and your boundaries. These markers make you who you are, and ultimately determine how you communicate, and participate, as an individual in society or in a relationship. There is no right or wrong here. Understanding the answers to these questions will help you understand why you behave the way you do, and how you respond to people around you.

1. What is your belief structure?

2. What is your heritage/culture?

3. What do you see is a lack of morals in today's society?

4. What was the worst thing that has ever happened to you?

5. What was the best thing that has ever happened to you?

6. Are you presently achieving your personal standards?

7. Are you where you want to be personally and career-wise?

Okay. Let us work through your answers. Does your belief system conflict with those around you? Does what you believe have any bearing on your decision-making or planning? Do your co-workers or friends know, either directly or indirectly, what your belief structure is? Is this having a positive or negative impact on how they work or relate to you?

Let us look at your heritage or culture. Are there rituals/customs that effect your schedule? Do other people in your life understand, or accept, these events? Do you get upset with others who do not share your heritage or culture? What weight do traditions have on your decision-making?

The first three questions, out of the seven listed, are designed to help you identify possible presuppositions that may exist consciously or subconsciously within you. These questions probe to the very core of your being. Understanding that your answers may, to a greater extent than you realize, affect how you are, and act, is an important skill.

Knowing that an individual has a different belief structure then you should never influence how you relate or treat that individual. Understanding that a specific heritage or culture is a personal thing, and not to be forced in any way onto another, will help reduce any feelings of prejudice that you may have. Learning about another person's heritage or culture can also be a rewarding exercise and will work toward eliminating any feelings of superiority that may exist within you.

If your moral standard is at a different place then another, and you notice a person performing what you deem to be immoral - this may lead to a personal confrontation. Everyone is at a different place in their lives, and whether you accept or reject what they may or may not do is not the issue. Being able to unconditionally accept an individual for who they are and not what they do, is a key to a healthy relationship.

In clearly identifying what the best and worst thing that has ever happened to you will help you understand why you may feel a closer bond to any particular individual. The people in your life may see that one of them has become your favorite, and that has upset those who are not your favorite. You may not see why they are seeing this and dismiss their behavior as their problem. The fact is that you may indeed be giving sympathetic or compassionate attention to a particular person without even knowing it.

As an example, if you had gone through a messy divorce or break-up, and you know one of your friends have just gone through one, or is going through a similar situation, you may subconsciously be giving that individual preferential treatment. You are responding to this person from your experience and feelings. This becomes dangerous as you naturally assume that this individual will go through all the same emotions and experiences that you did. The fact is that everyone will have a unique journey through the low times and the high times in their lives and pushing your journey onto them will end up overwhelming them and frustrating you.

This is a difficult skill to learn. The best support you can offer is to remain silent and listen. If you ended up sharing your experience as mentioned above, you have overpowered the individual going through their event, and replaced their experience with yours, making their experience obsolete, and your experience the primary experience. When the individual fights back to regain ownership of their experience, feelings of frustration and anger may emerge on your part, because they have not validated what you had experienced.

Answering the questions about where you are, and are you presently achieving your personal standards, will let you know quickly why you are reacting to your environment the way you are. If you see your job as unfulfilling or not challenging, then the number of times that you become impatient, crabby, or depressed, while at work, would dramatically increase. If you see your job as rewarding and fulfilling, this could help you understand why you would be impatient and frustrated with those co-workers who are just there for a pay check.

Personal standards are like trying to quit smoking, or generally becoming a better person. The list is endless as to the standards we set for yourself, and the list is endless as to the punishment you would inflict upon yourself for not achieving those standards. A pitfall with setting personal standards is the tendency to hold everyone around you to that same standard. This becomes upsetting to any individual, and to yourself - especially if you cannot achieve your own standard.

Do not misunderstand me. It is good to have high standards to strive after. Just understand that the process to achieve that standard could be long and agonizing. It is not worth beating yourself up if you fall, or make mistakes along the way, and it certainly will not help becoming disappointed in someone around you if they are not achieving your standards either.

For the next exercise, you will need to contact a close trusted individual. Ask him/her to give you a list detailing all of your good qualities. Meanwhile take the time to write out your own list of what you deem are your good qualities. You will find that for the most part your list will reflect what you perceive as your strengths, and the list from the trusted individual will reflect those ideal qualities of the good person that he/she sees in you.

Take some time to look over both lists. Take two items from each list that you most agree with and write them on a separate piece of paper. Now looking at each one of these four qualities you need to determine what your weakness is for each one. As an example, if one quality lists you as being a good provider for your family as a strength, a weakness might be that you work 50 or 60 hours a week.

Good Qualities	Quality 1	Quality 2	Quality 3	Quality 4
List them here:				
List the bad of each quality:				

Top two bad:				

After you have completed your list of the weaknesses of your strengths, spend a few minutes to put together an action plan. What steps can you start doing now that will help you improve your strengths? How can you measure whether or not you are being effective? Are there resources available to help you with your action plan? I would also recommend that you share your action plan with someone you look up to so he/she can provide ongoing constructive feedback to help you achieve your action plan.

The Bad

Now let's take a look at The Bad. Are not bad qualities relative? What may be good for someone may be bad for another, or vice-versa. Someone who exonerates that quality and is perceived as being successful would dispute any list of bad qualities. This then requires some explanation before you attempt to examine yourself looking for these bad qualities.

An objective approach is quite necessary as you naturally have a tendency to be blinded by your own brilliance. What you consider a strong quality or good quality may be vehemently denied by your spouse, partner, children, co-workers, or friends. It is through their eyes that you need to look, in order to see what they see.

Just as in a piece of twine where several pieces of string are interlocking and woven together so are your individual traits. The difficult part is if you recognize that one of those pieces of string is a bad trait it becomes agonizing to remove from the rest. What you find happens is that several of your good strings become unraveled and a process of rebuilding both your old good qualities and new ones needs to happen.

The reason why those good qualities become unraveled is that they were built around the dominate bad quality. When you objectively examine yourself to determine those good and bad qualities, you will most likely find that your good qualities are a fruit or offspring of a habitual or foundational quality. An example could be that you consider yourself to be a good listener and have always had an open-door policy. This is probably a habitual item given the fact that you have most likely always been a good listener right from your childhood.

The problem is that this good quality of being a good listener might be entwined with the tendency to own all of the problems that you hear about. You might find yourself lying awake at night thinking about the other person's problem. You may even catch yourself taking responsibility for the other person's problem, not that it becomes your fault that this person has the problem, but that it becomes *your* problem.

This does not mean that your good quality about being a good listener suddenly becomes a bad quality. What this illustrates is that a reflective process has to occur in order to determine why you tend to take over a problem. You may be overcompensating for a negligence that you had received. You may have had to deal with a huge problem in your life completely on your own and now have vowed to never allow an individual to go through what you had to go through. On the other hand, this could be the result of low self-esteem, or lack of confidence, in which you gain self-importance when you go on these problem crusades.

Taking an objective approach will prove to be very useful if you suffer from low self-esteem. In your effort to be modest or submissive, you would become a lot more critical of yourself. If you feel with every good quality that you may list, five people will be there to disagree with you so therefore you take that good quality and automatically turn it into a bad quality - stop. By stepping back

THE EXIT STRATEGY

and looking at this particular situation, you will be able to see what your bad quality is really, and it may not be what you thought it was.

Let us examine some interlocking or woven qualities in order to help clearly identify what a bad quality may be. In order to do this objectively, you need to first look at what a balanced person looks like. It would only make sense that anything that caused you to become unbalanced could be considered a bad quality. On the flipside, as I mentioned earlier, some of your good qualities may be the result of, or, fruit of a bad quality. Determining what makes a balanced person can help you address those bad qualities on which you have built yourself.

Imagine a perfect triangle with each side equal to the other. In the middle of this triangle is you. On each of the angles are three titles. These titles are (Spirituality, Belief Structure, and Personal Standards) – (Relationships with family, friends, and co-workers) – (Process, Ability to perform a job). A balanced person keeps each side of their triangle equal to the other. Any shifting of these titles and the person becomes unbalanced.

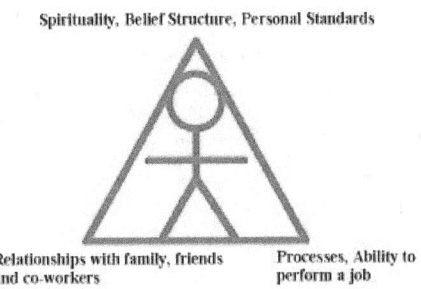

Too much of any of these could throw us off balance and create several bad qualities. Let us look at an example for each of the six combinations mentioned. After each one, take some time to record your thoughts surrounding each description. How much does each description describe you? It may be valuable to write down specific examples in which you can relate to each description. Remember the point of this exercise is to recognize your good qualities, which may be wrapped around a dominant bad quality. Understanding that what you will end up with is an unbalanced triangle will help you bring some balance back again to yourself.

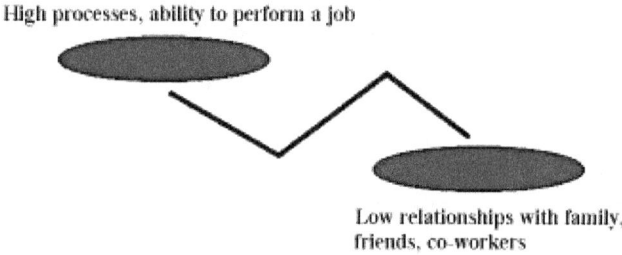

Enter **Dictator**. In your focus on doing the very best job, you run the risk of alienating your friends, your family and your co-workers. Your friends may suffer because all you share with them is about work and all the stresses that come with that. Your family may suffer because of the increased amount of time needed for you to do your job. Finally, your co-workers may suffer because of this dictator-type person barking criticisms at them all day long.

Answer these questions.

1. In what ways are you a dictator?

2. In what ways are you not a dictator?

3. Name a specific time that your co-workers would describe you as being a dictator.

4. Would your family say that time with them is suffering because of your commitment to your job?

THE EXIT STRATEGY

5. When was the last time that you spent quality time with your friends, family or your co-workers?

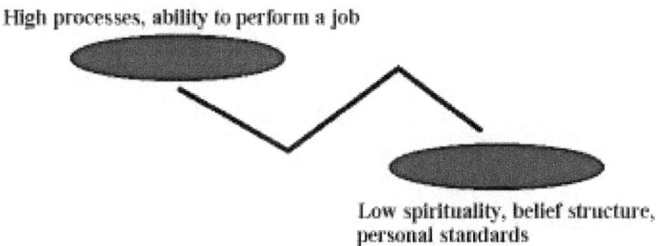

Enter **Denial and Condemnation**. In your focus on doing the very best job, you run the risk of burning yourself out or crashing under the weight of self-imposed condemnation. This is by far the hardest to recognize because of the fact that you can become comfortable with denial. When you start sacrificing a personal foundational belief or standard in which you had earlier determined who you are, you are setting yourself up for failure. Over the long-term, this type of imbalance leads to self-pity, depression, and bitterness, with a relentless pursuit of excellence in your job. This creates low morale in all your relationships, as they are no longer able to achieve your standards and resentment on your part as you start to lash out at most everything around you.

Answer the following questions:

1. Have you found that the times you are becoming irritable is increasing over the last couple of years?

2. How many co-workers have you worked with in the last year? How many have left either through their means or through being fired? Compare this to the total staff to determine the staff turnover.

3. If you determine that there has been a high staff turnover, are

you willing to look at yourself as a possible cause of that turnover, or the things that you might be doing to attribute to it?

4. When was the last time that you celebrated something specifically related to your personal beliefs or spirituality?

5. What conclusions are you drawing when answering these questions?

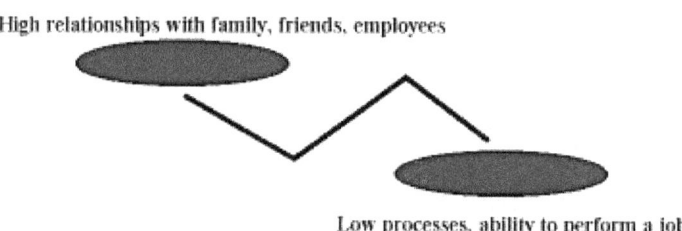

Enter **Everyone's Friend**. In your focus on having strong, healthy relationships with family, friends and co-workers, you run the risk of losing your ability to perform your job. You tend to avoid conflict and do whatever it takes to make those people, whom you deem important around you happy. Friends might keep you out late when you work early the next morning. Family may demand every long weekend off to go on family outings or co-workers may not respect you when you try to offer advice. The result, no matter what the situation, is that you may have artificially succeeded in making those people around you happy but you have now lost your job because you neglected those responsibilities.

Answer the following questions:

1. When was the last time that you offered work related constructive criticism to one of your co-workers? If longer than four months then why?

2. What type of response do you get from your co-workers when you try to introduce a new way of doing something or any suggestion for improvement?

3. How much time off has your family requested from you in the last six months?

4. Do you find that you have time to prepare for the demands of your job or are there limited time in your schedule?

5. Honestly assess your job performance. Has your overall productivity gone in a downward spiral over the last couple of years?

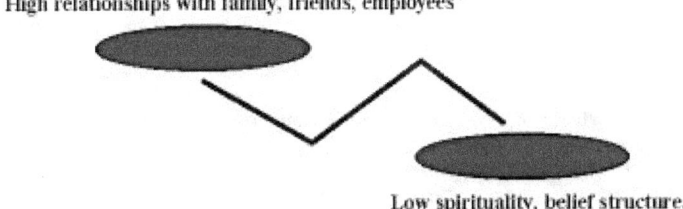

Enter **Peer Pressure**. In your focus of having strong, healthy relationships with family, friends, and co-workers, you run the risk of losing your identity. A typical, "Keep up with the Jones" mentality, has control over you, and will not let go until you are transformed to their liking. Unfortunately, in a typical example, once you have given up everything that makes you who you are, you may find that the very people you sacrificed yourself for are not there anymore. Do not lose sight of who you are, and do not compromise your foundational qualities for anyone. In the end, it is not worth it.

Answer the following questions:

1. Have you done something regrettable in the last year in order to gain someone's approval?

2. Examine your friends for a moment. How many of them have known you for longer than five years? How does this compare to the number of friends you have now?

3. Have you attended any social events with any of your co-workers over the last year?

4. How has this effected your working relationship with them? Would you be able to offer constructive criticism to them if necessary?

5. Are you driven by your own goals or by goals set by someone else?

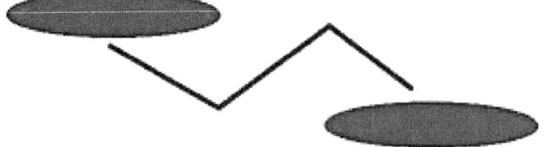

High spirituality, belief structure, personal standards

Low processes, ability to perform a job

Enter **Crusader**. In your focus on doing and living up to your personal standards and beliefs, you run the risk of over-challenging every process or philosophy in your relationships. This becomes an area of tension between your friends as well as your co-workers, and family. Instead of focusing on your job, or enjoying the relationships, you have decided to create issues around you, because you see the workplace, your friends, and/or your family as not complying or participating in your personal standard or belief structure.

THE EXIT STRATEGY

Answer the following questions:

1. List one business practice that your workplace does that you disagree with.

2. If you could change anything about the organization you work for what would that be?

3. Are there things that any of your friends or family is doing in their personal life that you disagree with?

4. What was the nature of your last conflict with your friend or family member? Who was right? Why?

5. How honest were you in answering these questions? If you were not, what were you trying not to draw attention to?

High spirituality, belief structure, personal standards

Low relationships with family, friends, employees

Enter **Preacher**. In your focus on doing and living up to your personal standards and beliefs, you run the risk of destroying those relationships around you. It is said that if you want to be an influence on someone then you must show and not say. You need to focus on the individual, and not what they may or may not be doing, or what they may or may not belief. This type of behavior could cause resentment, anger, and backlash from your co-workers, friends, or family, who do not agree with what you are saying. It could then lead to a serious breakdown of communication.

Answer the following questions:

1. Has there been a conflict in the last year with any of your co-workers, friends, or family that you believe they started?

2. Are there co-workers, friends, or family that comes from different races, beliefs or cultures? If so, how does their presence make you feel?

3. Over the last year, have you found yourself focusing more attention on an individual that you would describe as doing things, or believing things that would be contrary to yourself? An example would be something as simple as a friend that smokes when you do not, or as complicated as someone who has embraced spiritual practices that are contrary to your own.

4. When you enter into a social area of your workplace (as an example), do you find that the room goes quiet, or when you try to engage your friends in social conversation, the talk is usually shallow and short?

5. How would you describe your long-term objectives in relation to each of your co-workers, friends, or family? Take note of those that you want to end a relationship with, change, or modify in anyway. What is it about that individual that has contributed to you wanting to do any of these things?

With all of this information in front of you, I would like you to complete the following exercise. Contact that same trusted individual and request a list of all of your *bad* qualities. This will be difficult for that person to do because of their fear of somehow discouraging you. If this person's list seems too *fluffy* or inadequate in some way then I would encourage you to solicit this type of information from as many different sources as possible.

At the same time, complete your own list of *bad* qualities. Try to be as objective as possible using all of the scenarios of a *balanced* person.

Compare both lists and take the worst two from your list, and the other person's list. Examine all four qualities, and for each of the four qualities listed, write down your strength of each one. Now be careful that you do not write down the *fruit* of a bad quality. Use the example below as a guide.

Bad qualities	Quality 1	Quality 2	Quality 3	Quality 4
List them here:				
List the good of each quality				
Top two good				

Example:

On your list is the following bad quality; You avoid conflict and go out of your way to keep your co-workers, friends, and family happy. Now you may write, as your strength, that everyone enjoys being with you. This would be considered a *fruit* of being everyone's friend, but this is far from being positive from a personal perspective. When you need to face conflict, under this scenario, there will be much negative backlash from your co-workers, friends, and family.

What would happen if you decided to offer constructive criticism to a co-worker, friend, or family? Would there be any backlash? Would they show a complete lack of respect in your character? Would you find that you simply do not have a voice in these conversations, except to offer praise and positivity to them? In order to determine your strength of this weakness, you need to look at some foundational reasons for why you exhibit this *bad* quality. Going out of your way to keep these individuals happy can be considered a strength, but why do you do that?

Is this the result of past employers of yours that were tyrants? A childhood full of anger and unhappy memories? A broken relationship that has left you feeling lonely? Making your co-workers, friends, and family happy is a strength, but balancing that against your ability to express a constructive criticism, or to have your own voice in any situation, will require you to examine each of these questions carefully. You may find that you may have to learn some new tools, deal with past issues, or even research some new resources, in order to successfully build upon this strength and turn that *bad* quality into something positive.

The Ugly

Your dark side. For most people, these qualities very rarely are seen, and when they do emerge, it is because of a severe reaction to your immediate environment. There are some qualities or traits that from place to place, person to person, country to country, may be considered good or bad; depending on who you talk to. Unlike your bad qualities though, your ugly qualities are not relative and therefore cannot be watered down by popular opinion.

There tends to be a bit of ugly in each of us. These traits tend to stay inactive until their trigger is pulled. For some of us it would be increased stress, unresolved grief, a foreign environment, an attraction to a stranger, opposition to our leadership, or even encountering an upset person. The list is endless, and unique to each one of us, and the trick is to determine where that trigger point is.

When your ugly traits show themselves, they, for the most part, produce very noticeable results from those that are closest to you.

Some comments would include, "I just don't know you right now," "I don't like you like this," "What is wrong with you?" "Why are you acting this way?" Fortunately, for most of us we have these close relationships around us that will set off the alarm bells when an ugly quality emerges. What about the silent comments? What are people saying about you behind your back? Does the staff room fall silent when you enter? Is the dinner table a little less 'chatty' when you sit down? Is that social event a lot less quiet when you arrive? Do not judge how much or how little you show these ugly qualities just on the comments of a few; look at the silence of the majority.

So, what is an ugly quality? To begin, review your list of needs from the first exercise. Any personality trait that would attack these needs would be considered an ugly quality but it goes much deeper than that. No matter how conservative or how liberal an individual is, there is a list of basic human absolutes that cannot be denied as needs.

In examining how we participate in society, with each other, and how we react to our environment, we can find a common thread that weaves us all together. There are the three survival traits; being food, water, and shelter, as an example. This is common in every human being on this planet. Take away any of these from anybody and watch how they react. To bring it a little closer to home, watch what happens when one of these three elements is verbally destroyed or torn apart by an individual.

As an example, if an individual comes up to you and systematically takes you throughout your home pointing out every flaw structurally, and in all your stuff, and then at the end rattles off a list of why where you are living is completely not suitable, and inappropriate, how would you feel? It is not the fact that this person has made fun of the paint, or attacked the home in anyway, but the fact that this person attacked your ability to provide a suitable living environment. You have just been told that you are incapable of providing for yourself one of the three basics of human nature. In saying those comments, the individual has implied that you are inadequate and isolated from the rest of human civilization because of your gross negligence in providing shelter for yourself and/or your family.

There is another more precious list though. This list defines human existence, and it is a list that separates us from all the other species on the planet. It is these qualities, or needs, that no matter who you are, what you believe, or where you live; at the very core of your existence, you need these items. When an individual comes along and attacks any of *these* items, it is then when the ugly monster raises its head. This list can be argued that it is either too many, or not enough, when describing our needs, but I have found that for the vast majority of us, this list will cover them all.

Needs:

1. The need to be loved
2. The need to love
3. The need to know the truth
4. The need for acceptance
5. The need for a sense of worth
6. The need to be trusted
7. The need for friendship
8. The need for justification
9. The need for accomplishment
10. The need for protection or security
11. The need for knowledge
12. The need for understanding

Throughout our lives, we are constantly making choices, and doing things to provide ourselves with these needs. We become defensive, vulnerable, and emotional, when any of these needs are neglected, taken away, or criticized. Deep fulfillment occurs when any one of these needs are met. Are you, at times, the person that in any direct or indirect way, attacking the needs of one of your co-workers, friends, or family?

Trust becomes a huge issue when placed in light of all you have just read. When a co-worker, or friend, or family member, does not feel trusted then many of their personal needs are not being met, which creates a negative environment. The quickest way to re-establish good relationships and create a healthy environment is to trust. This can be the hardest thing for an individual to do, especially if a past experience of broken trust lingers.

Take a few moments to write down some names of co-workers, friends, and family, (preferably those whom you have a lot of contact with). Reflect on your relationship with each of them, focusing in on any existing or potential areas of conflict or tension. Spend some time objectively looking at each one to determine if the individual might have been looking to you to fulfill one or more of their fundamental needs, or if you indirectly or directly have threatened or destroyed one of those needs. What types of actions can you do to try and repair those relationships?

After taking this extensive look at yourself in preparation for not just The Exit Strategy but management in general I will now take you through a handful of basic management sections. As The Exit Strategy is all about engaging and developing the employee from recruitment through to termination I will begin with Interviewing as your first section that outlines the nuts and bolts of The Exit Strategy.

Interviewing

This is perhaps the most draining aspect of management because ultimately no manager has time to hire. Ideally, our workplaces are and will always be 'stocked' with great employees who have no desire at all to go anywhere and are willing to work whenever we need them to. But this is not the case and given today's work environment where more and more people are looking for jobs where the work environment is fun, engaging, and respectful of their contributions – instead of the money – you may find yourself constantly needing to recruit new employees.

This reality of employee turnover tends to frustrate the manager to a point where they are both equally bitter that they need to hire again and so worn out by the process that they end up hiring 'warm bodies' without any investment into the person. The manager simply wants this 'problem' to go away. However, the first challenge with the Exit Strategy is to understand that great management – great leadership begins at recruitment. What you do here – at the beginning of this journey for the applicant – will set you apart from the other managers.

Ironically, understanding these principles and practicing them well will ensure that the amount of times that you need to interview will dramatically decrease because study after study has told us – much to our chagrin – that an employee very rarely quits an organisation but instead they quit the person. And that person is most commonly you – their manager.

Take a look at the following checklist. Ask yourself the question and place a checkmark beside each of the answers that are applicable. This exercise will create an initial 'roadmap' for you in challenging some of your presuppositions around the hiring and recruitment process and shed some light on best practices when it comes to how you should approach interviewing.

For you, what is the purpose of the interview?[ii] (select all that apply)

- ☐ Hire someone to fill a job quickly
- ☐ Hire someone who is long-termer
- ☐ Hire a high achiever who's looking for a career move
- ☐ Screen out the weakest
- ☐ See if someone makes a good first impression
- ☐ Hire someone whom you like the most
- ☐ Hire someone who makes a great first impression
- ☐ If you're the hiring manager, demonstrate to the candidate that you're building a team of top performers, that you're an outstanding a leader, and someone a top performer would be honored to be part of your team.
- ☐ Prove to every candidate that you're smarter than they are
- ☐ Prove to every candidate that you're an important gatekeeper
- ☐ Determine if someone fits in the culture
- ☐ Determine if someone is technically competent
- ☐ Hire someone who's self-motivated
- ☐ Hire someone who possesses the four "A"s – affable, attractive and assertive, with good academics
- ☐ Demonstrate to the candidate that your company has high selection standards where every person hired is highly valued and they'll be working on high impact projects

THE EXIT STRATEGY

Now consider the following outcomes, as a result of the above:

- ☐ After a person is hired, how long does it take to determine if the new hire is fully competent to do all of the work required?

- ☐ How long does it take after the person is on board to determine if the person is highly motivated to do the work required without urging or excess direction?

- ☐ How long does it take to figure out if the new person consistently meets all performance objectives?

- ☐ How long after the person is hired would you feel extremely confident enough to recommend the person for a bigger job or to take over a critical project?

- ☐ How long does it take the new hire to realize what the job is fully about and wasn't misled?

If you're answers to any of the above are longer than a day, how can you possibly judge the person on these same factors in less than an hour? So, what is the real purpose of the interview? For most it seems the real purpose of the interview is to hire "90-day Wonders." These are people who are likable, outgoing, technically competent, and make good first impressions, but 90 days later you begin to wonder.

When you read a resume do not get bogged down with the details of the resume. Look for what is normally not there. Are they competent to do the actual work? You need to learn how to look for competence on a resume and how to listen for it in an interview. Are they motivated to do the actual work? There are signs to look for on a resume to help you answer that question. Does this person fit with the culture? By learning how to utilize conversational interviewing you can explore cultural adaptability with the candidate.

But before you even get to interviewing may I suggest the following procedure. This procedure works well in exploring organizational issues that are hindering the success of new employees as well as contributes to increasing employee retention rates.

Procedure When Posting A Position

These questions are meant to form an internal document that the Human Resource Department will provide to their supervisor. The purpose is to help the organization assess possible restructuring, process changes, identify necessary tools, and other foundational elements to help the organization move toward a higher retention rate with your staff.

1. Why is the position open? (person quit, new position, person terminated)
2. How long has the position been open?
3. Why did the last person leave this position? (explanation to question one)
4. What are the biggest challenges facing the new candidate in this position?
5. What are the three most important duties and responsibilities of this position?
6. What is the culture (atmosphere) of the department?
7. What is a typical day in the life of the new candidate in this position?
8. What training and education programs will you provide for this new candidate?
9. Is there room to grow in this position and the organisation?
10. Why do you like working here? (answer from your <manager> point of view)
11. How long have you been at this organisation, and how long have you been in your position?

In order to illustrate the purpose of this procedure let's examine Bill Hybels thoughts on building team[iii]. He talks about the four c's in building a team. They are Character, Competence, Chemistry, and Culture. When you think of one of your employees resigning, which of the three reactions below best describes you?

A. sigh of relief – 'phew' you see their resignation as a blessing – not because you don't like them, but maybe they weren't fitting, or they never became a member of your culture, or never performed at the level you hoped they would.

B. Would be a groan, 'ugh' this is someone who is a really good person, who's doing a good job, and they fit well in your culture. You don't want to lose a person like that, and now you have to find a good replacement, and that takes work.

C. A third response is that you run out and vomit. This is a fantastic person who's doing fantastic work, with a fantastic attitude and a fantastic fit with your unique culture. You would realize you might have lost someone who is, by human means, irreplaceable.

As managers you need to identify these employees that would make you vomit and then invest heavily in them long before they decide to quit you. Bill Hybel says, "We want to make a disproportionate investment in your talents. We want to develop you to your fullest potential. Tell us if there's ever anything that frustrates or demotivates you, because we'd like to fix it."

This process of team building happens at recruitment. If you approach the interview frustrated – only looking for a warm body to solve your temporary problem what you don't realize is that you are continuing to add to your problem. It isn't going away but in fact it is only getting worse. This is why the Exit Strategy focuses a lot of energy on this first step in the process – recruitment. It is recognizing that you have an unique opportunity at this first step to build a team that will last. Therefore, when you build your teams, you want to focus on the 4c's.

What is the *Character* of the person?

Is this person *Competent* in accomplishing what you have asked?

Do they have great *Chemistry* with you and with their teammates?

Do they understand your *Culture*?

This is where the skill of conversational interviewing is most useful. I will unpack conversational interviewing a little later on but for now simply understand that instead of approaching the interview in the antiquated manner of asking set questions on a sheet of paper in front of you, the idea is to engage the candidate in a meaningful conversation where they will begin to relax and open up to you.

When interviewing it is important to create enough space for a candidate to have a conversation with you. By creating space, you will help put the candidate at ease, encourage them to talk, build a good initial relationship and connection, and assess whether this person can fit well with the rest of the team.

Unfortunately, there will always be someone you need to say no to and it is important to communicate back to all the candidates you have interviewed as this communicates worth and value to them. How you say no to someone is just as important as celebrating yes to another. You need to shape your conversation to leave them a supporter of the organisation even though they are not going to be employed by you.

The Exit Strategy begins at recruitment. It takes the time to invest in every single candidate – in particular those chosen to be interviewed. The manager who uses the Exit Strategy will communicate worth and value to every person they interview and will work hard to make a supporter out of those they need to say no to. On the flip side the regular manager, frustrated that they even have to hire again and probably just as worn out will lean more toward the warm body method of hiring.

The problem with this unfruitful approach to recruitment is that you will most definitely end up with a warm body but you may also end up hiring an employee that very quickly reveals themselves to be toxic to your organisation[iv]. Let's examine what effect the toxic employee can have on an organisation so you can understand a bit better how important it is to get the hiring part right.

One is you will damage the trust each of your employees places on you to provide competent co-workers. If you indulge the negative behavior of the toxic employee and allow it to continue, chances are any trust the employees had in you and your ability to build a competent team will have eroded. Think twice before you gloss over behaviors which could be characterized as "acting out" or potentially damaging.

Next motivation from your current employees can plummet. As a manager when you ignore the toxic employee's actions you are seen as rewarding their negative behavior. What happens is that your inaction has lowered the bar when it comes to your expectation and the hard work that follows. Your employees – most often your top performing employees – will cringe at the fact that they now have to 'carry' this toxic employee, often through working disproportionately. Ultimately, you will risk having your top performing employees leave the organisation, all because of you ignoring the problem.

The toxic employee requires you to be vigilant and to pay attention to those nagging doubts or curiosities that quite often pop up early in the employee's probation period. They also can pop up in the interview process but your desperation to find a good employee sometimes clouds your judgment. By ignoring those feelings, you can do far greater damage later on to your entire team.

I am hoping that you now get a sense of how important the interview process is. When it comes to the art of interviewing the inexperienced manager begins their management career leaning more toward one end of the hiring continuum by bringing on board 'warm bodies' to do the job. This doesn't communicate worth and value to the candidate nor does it make a supporter out of those candidates you have to say no to. And as you have now just read it will inevitably end up with you losing your best employees.

However, there is a danger when the pendulum swings too far the other way. As you gain management experience you will also be gaining hiring experience but overtime this can also work against you. After time, and after reading hundreds of resumes there is a tendency to become one of the most cynical readers in the world. You will begin to realize that at least half of what you have read consists of lies, exaggerations, and half-truths. You no longer accept anything at face value.

All of these will end up skewing your outlook when it comes to recruitment. In other words, the potential is there for you to become cynical. You will begin to expect the worst and are not surprised when you get it. How I handle this personally is that I recalibrate myself every once in a while. I will purposely bring in a couple candidates that are at polar ends of the spectrum I am assessing resumes on. I do that to either affirm that I am still on the right track or to be pleasantly surprised and corrected in my skewed outlook and skewed screening.

Secondary Screening

After finishing the initial screening of applicants, you will have a smaller selection of resumes to consider. At this point I do secondary screening. The secondary screening is done via email. In the email ask the applicant to comment on the job description. This is a self-screening tool because if the applicant chooses to read it (many won't and that will be it) they may come across something in that job description that they feel would disqualify them. Good. That is what you want them to do as it helps screen down the applicants to someone who feels they are qualified or someone who really wants this opportunity to 'step-up'.

There are a number of reasons to do secondary screening via email.

1. You do not want to waste their time nor yours. So, although an applicant may look good you can gain additional information informally through an email interchange. Things like how long it takes them to respond to the email, the format of their response, or even how they respond.

2. It provides them with an opportunity to ask themselves if they really want to pursue this position, which is exactly what you want them to do.

3. It creates safety for them and when someone feels safe they tend to open up a bit more. You can then gain more insight as to who they are by allowing them the freedom to respond via email as they wish.

Preparing Interview Questions

Before you even have a conversation with a candidate make sure that it is because you think they can do the job, based on their resume and the pre-screening that you have already done. Do not waste your time or theirs by interviewing someone you are not already interested in. It is important that you are aware of their time and yours. This will also ensure that you remain curious about the candidate when interviewing them and that helps you maintain the conversational interview. It will also contribute to communicating worth and value to them throughout this part of the process.

Here are some typical questions that an interviewer will ask. It is followed by an explanation of the meaning behind the questions. The idea behind these examples is to demonstrate how limited these types of questions are when really you are desiring to understand so much more about the candidate. Through these examples it is my hope that you would be encouraged to move away from such narrow interviewing approaches and instead be motivated by a conversational style approach to interviewing.

Q: "Tell me a little about yourself."

The meaning behind the question: "I'm trying to figure out why you want this job and if you're a good fit." Typically, when the interviewer asks this type of question the candidate tends to answer it as if they were thinking you were interested in what they did over the weekend. The type of answer that you are looking for has a chronological, thematic structure. The candidate's answer should indicate that applying for this job was the next natural step. Therefore, in conversational interviewing it would serve you better to ask a question like, "I would like you to explain how your life experience, work experience, and educational experience has prepared you for this job".

Q: "What are your weaknesses?"

The meaning behind the question: "You're not perfect, so how do you compensate?" Note that recruiters are moving away from asking this question. In my opinion, such a question places the candidate on the defensive and erodes the quality of the interview conversation. Remember you must learn to intentionally communicate worth and value even in these conversations. I would use the opposite approach in conversational interviewing by asking a question like, "I see on your resume that you have accomplished a few really cool things. Could you spend a couple of minutes telling me about them?"

Q: "How do you handle stress?"

The meaning behind the question: "Do you have good problem-solving, time-management, and decision-making skills?" Typically, when the interviewer asks this type of question what they end up getting from the candidate is an answer to the question, "How do you unwind?" The type of answer that you are looking for is an example in self-care and healthy boundaries. As well their answer should reflect a moderate level of self-awareness. Therefore, a better conversation style question might be, "As you have read in the job description there are some aspects to this job that require some specific skills in order to make sure the employee doesn't burn out. Could you speak to those skills that you have acquired, which would benefit you in this job?"

Q: "What would others say about you?"

The meaning behind the question: "Are you a good fit for our team?" Typically, when the interviewer asks this type of question the candidate will most likely answer by explaining what their friends and/or their mom think about them, which is mostly unhelpful. You are looking for the candidate to reflect on the positive feedback they have received professionally. This will indicate whether they are connected well to previous employment situations, and whether they were able to build a supportive network while they were there. Therefore, a good question to ask in a conversational interview might be, "Could you speak to what you think our workplace culture might be about or how you hope it might be and how you see yourself fitting into that culture?"

Q: "Where do you see yourself in five (or ten) years?"

The meaning behind the question: "Do you know where you're going in life and are we a part of it?" Such a question is so standard in interviewing that it almost borders on entrapment. Any answer apart from complete loyalty to the organisation would be seen as a negative. In asking this type of question you would be looking for an answer that reflects a passion and goal-orientated person. This type of question and answer also tends to reflect how the person views themselves, which from a counseling perspective may be limited by the various external identities present in their life. Therefore, this candidate may truly be an all-star employee but their current view of themselves would limit them from seeing that. So, if you need to move away from asking these types of common questions. Where do you go?

Conversational Interviewing

Conversational interviewing is the method to create space for a candidate to have a conversation that will help put the candidate at ease, encourage them to talk, build a good initial relationship and connection, and assess whether this person can fit well with the rest of the team. Conversational Interviewing is the method in which you as the interviewer engage the interviewee in an open-ended conversation. You demonstrate curiosity for what they are saying, you use reflective listening techniques and open-ended questions in order to open up space for the interviewee to talk – ideally about themselves.

To do conversational interviewing well you need to first prepare for the interview. You need to examine the position you are interviewing for and determine three key questions that you can ask if you need to in order to move the conversation forward. These key questions must embrace the philosophy, culture, mission, and purpose of the position. It can touch on qualifications and objectives but those tend to generate canned responses and contribute negatively to the interview conversation.

Let's take a closer look at these three questions. In a more succinct way I can list the three questions this way.

Number 1: can you do the job?

Number 2: will you love the job?

Number 3: can I tolerate working with you (and conversely will they tolerate working with you)?

That's it. Those three. Each question potentially may be asked using different words, but every question, however it is phrased, is just a variation on one of these topics: strengths, motivation, and fit.

Let's unpack these three questions a bit more.

Can you do the job?

This is a focus on strengths. it's not just about the technical skills, but also about leadership and interpersonal strengths. Technical skills help you climb the ladder. As you get there, managing up, down and across become more important. Not only is it important to look at the technical skill set they have but also the strengths on what is called the EI (Emotional Intelligence) side of the equation in terms of getting along and dealing or interacting with people.

In other words this question will help you explore the candidate's personality. When drawn out using conversational method you can create the space for the candidate to answer questions like; How will they approach their work? Do they have the necessary drive? Do they have the right attitude to achieve the desired job results? When creating space for a conversation to happen pay attention to their personality and try to hone in on key indicators in what they say that may lead you to better understand who they are.

Will you love the job?

This question focuses on motivation. Study after study have showed that younger employees do not wish to get paid merely for working hard—just the reverse: they will work hard because they enjoy their environment and the challenges associated with their work. However, older employees want to be well compensated for a standard work done. Older employees normally bring a depth of experience and healthy skill set so a balance of the both is necessary on a team. Motivation for an older person may be the desire for others to learn from their experience and the opportunity to help this older person contribute in really meaningful and sometimes very tangible ways.

Embedded in this question is the intent to understand the candidate's cognitive ability. Will they be able to cope with the mental demands of the job? How do they solve problems? How will they communicate? As they describe more about themselves show curiosity in what they say and use reflective listening skills to help them expand on what they are saying. As they offer more meaningful explanations and attempt to answer your open-ended questions you will be able to gain more insight to their cognitive ability.

Can we tolerate working together?

A cultural fit is sometimes more difficult to determine. Some key indicators that may demonstrate that someone understands the culture is the following:

1. They are good friends / related to someone who works for your organisation
2. They have personal / professional experience with the services / products that the organisation provides
3. They have lots of volunteer experience in similar work situations
4. They have been a consumer / customer of the services / products that the organisation provides

This question is attempting to draw out the candidate's occupational interest. What type of activities will motivate and prompt candidates to succeed? In what type of culture or environment will they thrive? Not everyone who applies for a particular job wants to actually do that particular job. Sometimes the plan is to get their foot in the door and then quickly move into some other area. They will say what they think is all of the right things in order to accomplish that goal. You can gauge occupational interest in and through the way they have spoken about previous employment and to the depth of their understanding of the position they are applying for. A great question to gauge this if the conversation is stuck is to ask them to explain what they think the position is about that they applied for.

Once you have received answers to these three main questions ask yourself this question: How does the candidate's overall make-up compare to your best performers in the same job? Your take away at the end of the conversation with the applicant should be compared to a similar conversation you would have with your top performer.

If the candidate is anywhere in the same ballpark as your top performer you probably have a winner.

So, how do you have the conversation with the candidate using conversational interviewing skills? You start with asking open-ended questions not closed-ended. I love this example: "Can anyone give me an example of an open-ended question?"

Answer: "Yes". I just asked a closed-ended question.

Practice reflective listening as this invites the candidate to say more and demonstrates your interest. Reflective listening in its infancy is repeating back everything you though you heard the candidate saying. By reflecting back what you thought you heard the candidate saying it invites them to either agree or disagree. If they disagree they are invited to say more about their original answer, thus providing you with more information.

Draw out skills and talents that the candidate has shared and build on them. This puts the candidate at ease and invites them to share more information. This is affirmation in action. If the candidate speaks to some accomplishment, skill, or talent that they have you need to pick up on their sense of satisfaction around the item. What they focus on may have nothing to do with the job but it is an invitation for you to show interest – curiosity – and drawing it out helps create a sense of safety for the candidate, putting them at ease, and allowing them to talk more.

Try not to take any notes as this can be intimidating for the candidate. Show through your body language that you are truly engaged with what the candidate has to say – this communicates worth and value to them. If you take notes then make sure they are done in front of the candidate and that they are only positive things that you are curious about and want to ask when you have a moment. The reason for this is that we always remember the negative things so there is no need to write them down on a piece of paper.

Now let's talk about ending the conversation. It is important to pay attention to your intuition and respond to it as soon as possible. Your body language leaks what you are feeling and thinking all the time so if you are aware that the candidate is not a good fit for the organization then you need to pull the plug on the conversation immediately. Most of the time the candidate will sense that the interview is going poorly so provide them with a way to exit well.

Once you have given an interview I want you to feel obligated to communicate back to the candidate either a yes or a no. making a commitment to contact the candidate either way is honoring to them and respectful of their time. When you communicate a no – which can be done via an email, make sure that you communicate something positive that you reflected on out of the conversation with them.

Again, let them know that they had the right stuff as you had screened the applicants down from such a number to a precious few candidates. Save the yes candidate to the end of the process as it does make you feel good to be able to say yes to someone – so why not reward yourself after getting all the no's out of the way?

THE EXIT STRATEGY

Time Management

This chapter is not a ploy in order to get you to be more productive so you can be as good as Stan in accounting. Time management is not a comparison tool. Time management is really agreement management with yourself^v. At the end of the day, how good you feel about what you did (and what you didn't do) is proportional to how well you think you kept agreements with yourself. Time management is designed to help you when you are feeling overwhelmed, a bit in over your head, or buried under your desk somewhere staring at hundreds of emails hoping that your supervisor does not notice.

At the end of your day did you do what you told yourself to do? Did you accomplish what you think should have been accomplished? Wasting time only means that you think you should have been doing something other than what you were doing. Sleep is not a waste of time if you think you need it. Taking a walk instead of rewriting your year-end report is not a waste of time as long as you think taking a walk is the thing to do at that moment. It's when you wind up not having done that which you've agreed with yourself should be done that the trouble begins.

However, you still need to write that yearend report and you still need to deal with those emails staring back at you. You have people pushing against you from all sides, your work is piling up on your desk, and the phone won't stop ringing. Agreeing with yourself to take a walk when these pressing items surround you is not effective time management so what am I trying to say here? I am proposing a different way of looking at how you spend and utilize your time and the very first step in effective and productive time management is to understand how to work backwards from projects to goals to tasks.

The old method of listing the project at the top of your to-do list is a sure way to make sure you never get it done. Here are the steps to follow and then I will unpack the ideas behind these steps a bit more. The first step is to outline the project. Next is to breakdown the outline into smaller goals until you have specific tasks that can be accomplished in less than 90 minutes. What this process is explaining is something called a project list and what this process is not is something called a to-do list. Following these steps will help you accomplish your project without setting yourself up for failure.

I am not a fan of to-do lists. To-do lists are merely the vehicle of procrastination for the manager. Think about your current to-do lists. How often do you scan your list just so that you can pick off the ones you can finish in two minutes? How many items aren't really to-do's at all, but rather serious projects that require significant planning? It has been said that our brains can only handle about seven options before becoming overwhelmed. Think about ordering breakfast at a restaurant and note how quickly it takes you to become frustrated with the server's questions about our eggs, choice of potato, choice of bread, etc.

We are wired for pleasure and therefore when operating with a to-do list we are more inclined to take care of those items that only take a couple of minutes because it causes our brain to release dopamine – in other words it makes us happy. Try this out as a way of demonstrating how powerful this idea is: write out as many of your regularly daily tasks as you possibly can on a to-do list. Things like, turning on your computer, making coffee for the office, refilling paper in the photocopier, cleaning up the lunch room, organizing your desk, emptying your garbage. Fill your list with those types of items and then go do those things, however make sure that you pause to cross it off your to-do list once it is done and watch what that does to how you feel. You will feel really good but you have managed to accomplish no real work.

Throw away your to-do lists and let's begin to think of your tasks in a different way. When you look at your to-do list all you are reading are lines on a piece of paper. There is no context in which to understand the amount of work and more important – time – needed in order to accomplish those tasks. You may have a line item that says, "Review policy manual for approval" and the next line says, "Return Bob's email". You will naturally want to return Bob's email every time because of the sense of not really knowing or understanding the time commitment required to review the policy manual.

The other factor against these to-do lists is the lack of a commitment device. A commitment device is something external from yourself such as a project deadline from your supervisor that serves as an external motivation for you to accomplish said task. To-do lists are generated from yourself and is representative – albeit in a vague way – of what is left as tasks for you to do and therefore do not properly reflect those external motivations. Your supervisor's project simply becomes a sentence on your list that gets buried. The reason it gets buried is because you are constantly adding to the list with new tasks and there is no context as to understand the priority behind each new task. This lack of commitment device therefore renders your to-do list ineffective.

Here is the fix. Determine what items on your to-do list are a project and not a task. Break that project down into smaller goals and then break those goals down into tasks. Instead of one sentence you will now have several line items. Now estimate how much time each of those tasks will consume, and transfer them to your calendar. Immediately you will see that your perspective has changed. You have gone from a piece of paper beside your phone that lists all of these projects to a more realistic and achievable approach through daily and weekly planning.

However, when planning out your day don't forget to leave time to process your email. In addition, leave some empty space – one or two hours – each day to deal with the inevitable crises that will crop up. As you move from a to-do list to a project list you will need to decide which item to handle at what time as you plan your day and your week. This overcomes the paradox of choice and provides a commitment device to help you do the right thing at the right time.

It's an eye-opening exercise: you'll probably find that it's tough — if not impossible — to find a place for everything. After completing this exercise, you have now used the calendar to paint a true picture of the time commitments you have on your plate. Putting your work in the calendar enables you to better determine whether or not you can (or should) say yes to a new project. And if you do say yes, you can better determine when you realistically might be able to get it done. You might think, "There's no way I could tell my boss that I can't do this by mid-February." But I'd argue that you have to say no. You have the responsibility — to set expectations about what can be accomplished with the amount of production time you have available.

Multi-Tasking

I purposely do not even attempt to multi-task as I am convinced that accomplishing one task at a time helps me produce much higher quality work in a shorter amount of time then my colleagues who are praised for being a multi-tasker. In fact I would go as far as to say those who claim to be best at multitasking are actually the worst at it. At least that's the finding of a University of Utah study[vi] that looked into whether those who multitask most are actually better at switching between tasks than the rest of us. Turns out they're not better. They're worse.

"What is alarming is that people who talk on cells phones while driving tend to be the people least able to multitask well," psychology Professor David, a senior author of the study, commented. "We showed that people who multitask the most are those who appear to be the least capable of multitasking effectively."

"The people who multitask the most tend to be impulsive, sensation-seeking, overconfident of their multitasking abilities, and they tend to be less capable of multitasking," co-author David Strayer said, elaborating that "people multitask because they have difficulty focusing on one task at a time. They get drawn into secondary tasks. … They get bored and want that stimulation."

Fascinated by this claim I examined the source study and found the following information. In 80 clinical trials, it was found that the IQ of those who tried to juggle messages and work fell by 10 points - the equivalent to missing a whole night's sleep and more than double the 4-point fall seen after smoking marijuana.

"We have found that this obsession with looking at messages, if unchecked, will damage a worker's performance by reducing their mental sharpness." The author of the survey said the IQ drop was even more significant in the men who took part in the tests.

Therefore, the next big idea that I need to blow up is to stop multi-tasking. No, seriously – stop. Switching from task to task quickly within the same context of time does not work. In fact, changing tasks more than 10 times in a day makes you dumber than being stoned. When you're stoned, your IQ drops by five points. When you multitask, it drops by an average of 10 points, 15 for men, five for women (yes, men are three times as bad at multitasking than women). So, your first big challenge was to stop using to-do lists and switch to project lists. Now your next big challenge is to stop multi-tasking.

By planning out your project list you will no longer need to multi-task because you have factored in those external commitment devices. In other words, you know when the deadline is on a project, you have broken that project down into smaller goals, followed by breaking it down into achievable tasks. You have then assigned a time value to each of those tasks and have inputted them into your calendar. Then each day you work for a set amount of time accomplishing one task at a time until those tasks eventually lead to the project being completed.

The multi-tasker will have their desks cluttered with many different projects going on at the same time and at best – if the projects are delivered on time they will not be reflective of their best work but of work barely completed. More importantly the risk to the manager who multi-tasks is that they will not be in a position to understand their limits – to be able to push back and say no when and where needed on projects. Instead, they will be fighting discouragement and potential burn-out as a result of bouncing from one thing to another. In the life of a multi-tasker there is never an opportunity for the dopamine release from truly accomplishing tasks as they are too distracted and too busy focused on the next thing.

Email

Although our email programs have become incredibly powerful over the years, namely through integrated search bars that allow the computer to search through our thousands of emails for us, there is still a physiological stressor attached to staring at a screen that is completely out of control. As email is simply an in-box, it needs to be emptied regularly to be functional. "Empty" does not mean finishing all the work outlined in your emails – it means making decisions about what each one means and organizing it accordingly. The same procedures apply to any in-box – whether it's the tray on your desk or your answering machine. They should be processing stations, not storage bins.

It takes less effort to start every day or two from zero in your in-box than it does to maintain "unstructured blobs" of accumulated and unorganized "stuff" that must continually be re-read and re-assessed for what they mean. Even though you can conduct an email search for what you are looking for the search results will only return a grouping of emails requiring you to spend additional time wading through the virtual mess you have created for yourself.

Your emails provide you with bits of information that are either responses to inquiries or are inquiries themselves. Collectively they represent those dreaded to-do lists but instead of one piece of paper filled with lines of items to be accomplished imagine hundreds of these lists strewn randomly around your desk. Unorganized emails act like those lists and so if you are going to become more efficient in your time management you must learn how to file your emails. Make reference folders in your navigator bar and file similar kinds of emails over there. It's a lot easier to lose track of them among the five hundred or a thousand in your in-box than with a label you can name. One simple alpha-sorted list – by topic, theme, or person – is usually sufficient and easier to deal with.

Purge emails when you have little windows of time. If you are waiting for an appointment, or a phone call, or you completed a task a few minutes before you break for lunch – these are golden opportunities to deal with the numerous emails clogging up your inbox. The general rule of thumb in order to maximize your productivity in these precious few moments is to complete the less than two-minute ones. Anything you can deal with in less than two minutes, if you're ever going to do it at all, should be done the first time you see it. It takes longer to read it, close it, open it, and read it again than it would to finish it the first time it appears.

Organize emails that require action and follow-up. If you've deleted, filed, and finished your two-minute emails, you're left with only two kinds: (1) those that require more than two minutes to deal with and (2) those that represent something you're waiting on from others. A simple and quick way to get control is to create two more labels in your navigator bar – "Action" and "Follow-up" and file them accordingly. These labels should be visually distinct from your reference labels and should sit at the top of your labels list, which can be accomplished by making them all caps with a prefix punctuation like the @ symbol or a hyphen (whichever will sort the labels to the top).

It is much easier to assess your workload with actionable emails organized in one place. Do not forget to consistently review actionable emails. Once you get your in-basket to zero, it will feel fantastic. However, remember that you can't ignore the batch of action emails that you have organized. You will need to develop a good habit of checking on them regularly to feel okay about what you're not doing with them at the moment. Make sure to keep actionable and non-actionable emails in separate places. In summary, keep your inbox empty. Delete what you can and purge your reference files regularly, as things get out of date and lose their value to you. Remember to keep your actionable emails reviewed.

In addition, be good at the keyboard as being a slow typist will always be a hindrance to your ability to manage your time efficiently. Not only is poor typing speed inefficient, it creates a resistance to engage with email that undermines all the best intentions to get on top of it. If you're not up to at least fifty words per minute, getting there with a good typing tutor could make a world of difference.

Schedule your email. Pick two or three times during the day when you're going to use your email. Checking your email constantly throughout the day creates a ton of noise and kills your productivity. Pick a time to review your emails and stick to that routine. As a suggestion you can check them when you arrive in the morning, after lunch, and just before you leave work for the day. In order for this to be successful you need to be able to have your emails organized, following the practical tools we have just reviewed.

Self-Care

Over the years I have found a direct link between self-care and time management, meaning if I focus on self-care as the priority I find that I can increase my productivity. My conclusion is that I have found that in order to be really good at self-care one must really focus on time management at the same time. As an example, since moving away from to-do lists to project lists, an important part of the project list is to remind yourself of the milestones accomplished on your way to completing the project. Celebrating those goals helps reinforce the dopamine connection to a task completed and rewards your mind of effective methods utilized in order to get the work done. This type of positive reinforcement comes out of early childhood development methods where positive reinforcement ensures that the child will do the expected behavior again. You are in a sense patting yourself on the back and that is a wonderful way to train yourself to implement similar strategies again on the next project.

When you are early in your attempts to put in place some effective time management methods remember that you will make mistakes. You will. You will not be able to avoid that. Therefore, it is important to remember to learn from your mistakes. Identifying what you can do differently next time can help you reach your goals. If you are not learning from our mistakes then you are falling into the old saying, "The definition of insanity is doing the same thing over again and expecting different results".

Self-care in the workplace also involves three key aspects of business communication. The first key is to remember to ask good questions. There can be a lot of stress connected to communication in the workplace and consequently where stress is present the ability for self-care is challenged, which will directly impact your ability to have effective time management. You need to learn the art of asking good questions. Ask a good question and you get a good answer. The opposite is also true. In addition with good answers you can make good decisions, which will impact what you do in a successful way.

The second key is to understand how your progress is being monitored. You do this by understanding how the person whom you report to is monitoring your progress. By making sure the two of you are on the same page, and then you adjusting your goals and objectives in order to show progress will in fact be the fastest and most effective method of achieving this goal and finding success. This contributes to your self-care because you are eliminating key points of stress in key workplace relationships.

The last key is to communicate effectively. Whether you're asking for help, delegating a task, or teaching others, you need to get your point across clearly. And speaking of asking for help as a primary way of self-care in the workplace please remember to ask for help. Don't be afraid to seek help. You cannot do it on your own. That is why you are part of a team. Self-care realizes that you cannot do everything on your own and learning how to ask for help at key moments will help contribute to a positive work atmosphere. I am a firm believer that the more positive we can make the workplace the more productive it will be.

A couple more thoughts surrounding self-care. First, change your environment at least once during the day. Go for a short walk during a break or meet with someone outside of your office. If you are working on a project – try setting up a different location in which to do the preliminary work on the project. As an example, meet with an employee in a different room other than your office.

Take real and regular vacations. Real means that when you're off, you're truly disconnecting from work. Regular means several times a year if possible, even if some are only two or three days added to a weekend. The research strongly suggests that you'll be far healthier if you take all of your vacation time, and more productive overall.

Overwhelmed?

May I suggest that if you are reading this and you are still feeling overwhelmed in this area of time management then perhaps the problem is to acknowledge that you cannot do it all. The idea that you will eventually get caught up is a myth. It's impossible. You have more work than you can reasonably expect to get done. And unfortunately, your workload is not static. Even now, while you are reading this chapter, your inbox is filling up with emails.

When feeling overwhelmed with all of the tasks laid out before you, covering your desk, filling up your email, blowing up your phone an effective solution is to practice workload triage. You must know which things you can safely ignore and which things demand your intervention. On the battlefield, medics have to decide where to apply their limited resources. They can't help everyone. triage is the process of sorting victims, as of a battle or disaster, to determine medical priority in order to increase the number of survivors.

Some patients will survive without medical care. Some won't survive even if they have medical care. Triage means ignoring these two groups and focusing on those that will only survive with medical care. This triage terminology is used in an effort to illustrate the need to task yourself appropriately. Let's take a look at how you might prioritize time. The majority of employees feel that deadlines mobilize their best skills. So what tasks are assigned to you that come with timelines? What tasks do you wish came with timelines so it can help both motivate you and help you organize your time? Your supervisor needs that information.

Here is a popular strategy for time management. Start with categorizing your tasks by priority. A – urgent and important. B – important but not urgent. C – urgent but not important. D – not urgent or important. At the beginning of each day, focus on A's first. If you get those done, move to the B's, then the C's.

There is a debate among time management specialists as to whether one should prioritize or not prioritize. To reflect my own journey in time management I can tell you that when I started learning time management I found that prioritizing my tasks was helpful. However, as the years went by and I became more proficient at what

THE EXIT STRATEGY

I was doing I eventually stopped prioritizing my tasks.

I now work on a Tetris strategy in the sense that I have an idea how long it will take me to complete each of my tasks and I schedule them in accordingly as to maximize how productive my day is. With a priority list – that approach does not factor in the amount of time needed to accomplish the task, which in of itself may interfere with the flow of your day rendering your ability to manage your time effectively – non-effective.

This is because you need to find a balance between time as a restraint of your work day and task management. In order to have really effective time management skills and consequently become very productive with your time you need to not just prioritize your tasks utilizing the triage example earlier but by also balancing that against the Tetris principle. As an example if you start your work day with a priority A task that you know will take two hours to complete but you have a meeting in 45 minutes then a better use of your time would be to identify a task that you can accomplish in 45 minutes. You are choosing to accomplish a task in 45 minutes instead of starting then stopping only to have to come back to your priority A task later, which becomes a very ineffective approach to time management.

Still overwhelmed? Practice intentional neglect instead of unintentional neglect. Unintentional neglect is the person who forgets to do something or they are late in meeting their deadlines. This inevitably happens if you don't practice intentional neglect. You must decide in advance you will not do category D tasks. They are neither urgent nor important. They are simply not worthy of your time or attention.

"But," you may ask, "what about tasks I don't think are important but someone else does?" Great question. Let me give you an example. Each of us will have someone we answer to within the organisation and we need to understand that our supervisor's priorities need to become our priorities. When I unpack the concept of Blue Chips later in the book you will learn how to do that in detail but in the moment, it is enough to chew on the idea that your supervisor's priorities need to become your 'A' priorities.

Multi-Tasking Is A Myth

So how do we overcome overwhelmed-ness? You do the next most important thing next. Multi-tasking is a myth. You really can't do more than one thing at a time – at least more than one thing that requires focused attention. Get your list of priorities. Do the most important thing first, then move to the next item and work down your list. Effective time management is coupled with productivity. This is how you measure effective time management. It is on this principle that you will discover that multi-tasking as a way of being more productive is a myth.

Tell the truth: Do you answer email during calls? Do you bring your laptop to meetings and then pretend you're taking notes while you surf the net? Do you eat lunch at your desk? Do you make calls while you're driving, and even send the occasional text, even though you know you shouldn't? Between 25% and 50% of people report feeling overwhelmed or burned out at work. We spend too many hours juggling too many things at the same time. The biggest cost is our productivity. When you switch away from a primary task to do something else, you're increasing the time it takes to finish that task by an average of 25 per cent[vii].

We live in this modern age where we are bombarded with multiple sources of information all at the same time. Our phone prompts us wanting attention – our watch does the same, our computers show 100 new emails in our in-box, there are people knocking at our office door and our supervisor wanted the project we are working on done yesterday! It is hard enough to bring about order from these external devices in an effort to become more proficient at time management but easy for us to impose these very same distractions on those who report to you.

Effective time management also means you become aware of your external actions. Stop demanding or expecting instant responsiveness at every moment of the day from your staff. It forces your employees into reactive mode and makes it difficult for them to sustain attention on their priorities. Let them turn off their email at certain times. If it's urgent, you can call them – but that won't happen very often. When you ask someone in an email or in person to do something – give a reasonable time frame in which to respond. Our expectation for instantaneous results is a reflection of our society and one we need to actively push against for the sake of those who report to us and even for ourselves!

Do the most important thing first in the morning. Preferably without interruption. For 60 to 90 minutes, with a clear start and stop time. If possible, work in a private space during this period, or with sound-reducing earphones. Resist every impulse to distraction, knowing that you have a designated stopping point. The more absorbed you can get, the more productive you'll be. This idea of doing the most important thing first in the morning (going back to the idea of prioritizing your tasks) is very important. Study after study points toward this time of day being the most productive for all of us. If your day begins with you 'jumping right into it with both feet' and you are running right of the starting block you will fizzle out like a firework eventually becoming very ineffectual with your tasks.

Organizing Your Workspace

Good time management also means good space management. If your office is looking like it should appear on a show that focuses on hoarding problems may I suggest that your time management skills are probably being challenged as well. Or if you seal all sources of wind out of fear that your well organized stacks of paper all over your desk may be compromised then once again I am suggesting that perhaps your time management skills are not being fully utilized.

In order to be fully successful at time management you need to create an environment in which you can thrive. When you govern this space wisely it can be a place that allows you not to be busy, but productive. A little organization goes a long way in producing great outcomes. So, let's look at how to organize your space.

The workspace should function like the interior of a well-designed sports car – all the controls easily accessible as required, allowing for maximum focus on the work at hand, quick over-viewing of work to be done, and easy processing of all forms of input (from email, paper mail, phone, and live conversation). Here are some practical ways to organize your workspace[viii]:

A physical in-basket. (For an in/out basket system have the in-basket the top basket if you stack them). This is for your priority tasks in paper form. What this means is that your priority tasks should be at the top of your paper pile, not shoved to the bottom. In a similar way you need to set your email up along with your documents on your computer with an electronic in-basket. In your email that could be as simple as creating a folder that is labelled 'follow-up' but with an 'a' at the beginning of the name so it appears at the top of your folder list. An in-basket on your computer could be something as simple as a folder on your desktop that says 'follow-up'. Next you need a physical out-basket. You need some place where you can put the documents that need further action (such as filing or mailing) but are not important to do in the moment.

Make sure your office is equipped with some capture/communication tools. This would include a writing pad, stapler, tape; desk tray and holders for pens, post-its, paper clips, scissors, stamps. This includes some personal supplies, which are best kept in at-hand drawers. These drawers would include refills for writing instruments, batteries, business cards, stationery, envelopes, headphones, blank CDs or flash drives, small tools, and the like.

My office is set up with an inbox on a shelf above my computer to the left and then to the right is my outbox (to be filed items). My phone is right beside my computer. In my first desk drawer I have the capture/communication tools and in my second drawer I have the personal supplies. On the wall in front of me I have a telephone listing summary page and an account listing along with the organizational chart – some basic referral tools that I use frequently in the course of my duties. I have a cupboard which holds supplies such as envelopes and file folders. Everything mentioned here I have within my arms reach.

Your workspace needs to be functional. There are two types of materials that belong in your workspace and it's very productive to sort them accordingly. The first is what belongs there permanently and the second is what is in transit and incomplete. You need to be critical of your work space in order to determine what has action required and what doesn't, because it belongs there. You need to sort out what stays where it is and what still needs attention. Often, too, there are many things that should be purged out of the environment. Sometimes a plethora of outdated "stuff" can accumulate, clogging up drawers and nooks and crannies of desk real estate.

The only items that belong permanently in your workspace are: supplies, reference material, decoration, and equipment. Anything else goes first in the in-basket to be processed and then is either tossed, filed, or coded into your action-reminder system. An example of supplies is everything you need, and use up, on a regular basis such as writing and printer paper, stamps, paper clips, tissues, ink, etc. Reference material refers to your files, ring binders, directories, manuals, lists of codes, etc. Decorations could be wall décor, art, plants, family pictures, nostalgia, cartoons, etc. Equipment references furniture, phones, computers, printers, stapler, letter opener, pens, chargers, projectors, briefcases, etc.

Keep it current. Many things that start out as functional in those categories become outdated, useless, or misplaced simply by the passage of time. If you have things still around that you're not sure if you might need again (such as miscellaneous electronic accessories), consider putting them further away from you in plastic storage bins labelled "misc. gear", which you can then re-evaluate later as to its relevance. It's good to regularly purge and reorganize the desk, drawers, shelves, countertops, and files. It's very easy to be unconscious to stuff just because it's there, undermining the sense of active usage the item may have in your environment.

Let's take a look at your filing. It is important to pay attention to the logistics of filing in your office area because, besides furniture, it requires the most space and physical movement to execute. This is also important on our computers. Think about how you file information on your computer. How are you using your file folders? When you need critical information is it at your fingertips or do you need to go 'digging' for it through endless folders located in various places on your computer?

General reference filing (also including support files for projects in progress) should be within easy reach. Any reference material that can stand up by itself goes on your shelves, like books, thick manuals and binders (appropriately labelled). Anything else should live in its own file alphabetically in your filing cabinets.

The in-basket and your email should all be easily process-able while you're on hold on a conference call or waiting for someone to walk into your office. The in-basket can and should hold everything that is not yet organized, so there is no need to have a "messy desk". Of course, a legal pad or some form of easy note-taking device should always be right at hand in case the phone rings or you want to check voice mail, or someone pops into the office and lets you know something that you might want to do something with later on.

The action-reminder tools in a workspace consist of a calendar, reminders, and overviews of projects and longer-horizon outcomes. This might be project files or summaries either printed or electronically stored. The first thing usually accessed at hand is the calendar (and a clock), to let you know where you have to be today. It signifies the "hard landscape" for your day, and so must be the most easily and consistently reviewed device and information. The next most accessible for review need to be the action-reminder lists, folder, or baskets. ("Gee, I don't have to be in the meeting for another 15 minutes... what could I handle and get off my plate between now and then?")

For an example you could open up your electronic calendar and leave it open. Therefore, each morning when you come in you have a visual clue as to what your day is going to look like and how that looks in context to your week and your month. If you use Google Calendar each morning it can send you an email of all scheduled appointments and events, which serves as an additional reminder. When you use your note pad as a random place to scribble down action items that you can't immediately get to – to which you place in your inbox at the end of your day – you would grab this piece of paper at the beginning of your day in order to gauge what adjustments you may need to do in order to be the most productive with your time on this particular day.

Summary

Jim Rohn (a motivational speaker) said, "Either you run the day or the day runs you." He's right. Unless you want the day to run you then take control of your schedule and stick to it. A well scheduled day will go a long way in preventing distractions that would otherwise rob you of your productivity. The best call-screener or "drop-in" visitor deterrent you have is a well-maintained schedule. It will keep you from succumbing to the "tyranny of the urgent" and focused on your goals.

Work in 60 to 90-minute intervals. Your brain uses up more glucose than any other bodily activity. Typically, you will have spent most of it after 60-90 minutes. That's why you feel so burned out after super long meetings! So, take a break: get up, go for a walk, have a snack, do something completely different to recharge.

I talked about the most productive part of the day being first thing in the morning and the need to do what is important in the first 60-90 minutes. However, what you learn here is that this same pattern needs to repeat itself throughout your entire day. You are most productive when you break up your tasks into these smaller timeframes. Therefore, not only should you take a break after these time increments but you should also change what you are working on after each interval in order to generate the most productivity out of your time.

In the same way that you have taken your projects and broken them down into tasks, approach your week in the same way. Assign a day of the week to one specific job responsibility that you have. Refer to your job description for help with this. This does not mean that you will necessarily use the entire day for that one task but that it is your primary focus for that day. Take a certain amount of time, set aside and most efficiently near the end of your week to reflect on your past week's goals. What type of progress did you make through the week in order to meet those project deadlines? Make a rough plan and include any readjustments to your schedule now before you are back at your desk Monday morning.

In order to help you stay on course regarding those projects you are working on - utilize technology. Today's technology focuses on connectedness so use it to your advantage. If you are working on a project make sure that your project is digitally stored and updated instead of wondering whether or not the piece of paper in your hand is the most recent draft of the letter or not.

Make sure that you are constantly practicing good communication.

When you have an assignment or a task that your supervisor is waiting on do not make them remind you about it and do not ask for extensions. If you have questions ask them well before the deadline. If you do not have a deadline, ask for one. If you need help from other staff members actively engage them. Do quality work and turn it in on time.

Effective time management is severely eroded if you do not show up on time. Most times we are known by what we do rather than what we say. If you want to practice good time management then starting with this basic principle is a good place to start. If you are rushing in late for work or barely on time then I can also guarantee that it will take you at least half an hour before you are ready to focus on your first tasks of the day. Not only is that poor time management that is also poor stewardship and on the extreme end that could also be called time theft.

Another factor that works against all of us in practicing good time management are unnecessary meetings. For those meetings which are necessary, assure an agenda is set with a time allotment for each item on the agenda, the start and end times of the meeting, the purpose and the result desired. Stay within those parameters. In addition, it is important to share minutes from the meetings with all the participants and to refer to those past minutes before calling another meeting. You will find that these extra communication checks will contribute to minimizing how many meetings are necessary.

As you become more and more efficient with time management planning you will begin to understand how much of your time a newly assigned project will take. In this process there will be moments where it is very necessary for you to say no. Many times people get themselves into a time crunch because they simply are not willing to say no. And stick to your guns —no means no! Yes, of course, there are diplomatic ways of saying no and that is advisable at all times. Saying no could be seen as the first sign toward establishing healthy boundaries and maintaining good self-care.

As you grow in your efficiency in planning out your week by assigning tasks to each of the days with a Friday review of your week it would be ideal to move yourself toward scheduling a year in advance. To give you an idea, say a program summary is due every year on June 30. May 22nd, review of year highlights that you want to include in your report and have the first draft written. April 1st, begin writing the first draft and schedule some time each week to make sure you have it completed. March 21st, review your budget to get a sense of your financial picture heading into the final quarter. Put these dates into your calendar under recurring events. Adjust as necessary. This works no matter what job you hold —everyone has recurring events in their work.

Make sure that you return emails. There's no excuse for leaving your email unanswered for more than a day or two. Don't know the answer? That's no excuse to leave the email sitting in your inbox. Write a quick response anyway: "Hi Jan, I'm not 100% sure about this, so let me look into it, and I will get back to you by the end of the week." Then, get back to her before the end of the week. I'm not saying you need to answer every email the moment it arrives in your inbox however as I discussed earlier deal with every email immediately that will require less than 2 minutes to complete will increase your productivity and lend to good time management skills.

Make sure that you follow through. Do what you say. In order for you to improve your time management you will require clear instructions and perimeters from your supervisor. However, you also need to model this to those who report to you. If you make a commitment then make sure you complete that commitment when you said you would. This type of mutual accountability can serve as a great tool to help each of us improve our time management, simply out of obligation to follow through with what you said you would!

The last tip is to loosen the belt of your schedule. Ensure your scheduling is not so tight as to be constantly derailed by unexpected events. The only time you are guaranteed not to be sidetracked or derailed in your attempt to complete your tasks is if you have no contact with people. As an example, I will schedule only morning meetings or afternoon meetings but vary rarely will I schedule both on the same day. This provides me with enough time to deal with the expected 'unexpected' that will pop up and land on my desk.

Blue Chips

Blue chips found their meaning and use in the world of big corporate business or stock portfolios. It is a phrase meant to draw your attention to those key items within your organization that you should spend the most amount of attention on. Generally speaking blue chips for any organization are those key pieces of information that best represent how the organisation is doing. A fancy term for them are 'Key Performance Indicators'. However, success is measured in many different ways within any organisation and this is where the term blue chips comes in. Blue chips will vary from department to department within that organisation.

Blue chips are driven by your supervisor and consequently their supervisor. The blue chips represent bits of information that help inform your supervisor on how well your area of responsibility is doing. They are key communication points where you are expected to gather and report on each of those points on a regular basis. More than just reporting you are expected to have these key communication points (blue chips) available at your fingertips at any given moment and able to speak to them in detail when called upon.

Blue chips represent those larger defining tasks of your work environment. For every project that you work on you need to keep your blue chips in mind and be aware of how they may impact your project. Your supervisor needs to have access to that information at any time and it is your responsibility to make sure they can get access to that information (blue chips).

Now before I unpack this concept of blue chips let's get an idea of what you think blue chips might represent. Here is the exercise. Take a blank piece of paper. Write the title of your department at the top of the page. Write down no more than 5 blue chips for your department. In order to determine what the 5 blue chips for your department might be you need to look at your department from the perspective of the whole organization. In other words what do you think is important for the organization as a whole to know about your specific department?

To help you answer that question let me unpack the goal behind blue chip reporting within most organizations. I have broken it down by their primary departments as that will help inform your determination of your blue chips. This is because your blue chips must contain information points that are relevant to each of these primary departments.

The first department is the governing board via the head of the organisation. In corporate business that may look like providing data to corporate head office via the general manager. In a non-profit that would look like providing data to the board of directors via the executive director. In a smaller business structure that may look like providing data to the owner via the head manager or supervisor. It is important to note that in most cases the data you are providing under this example has already been predetermined by the owner or governing board. This may include things like monthly or quarterly sales figures, actual versus forecast numbers, or budget summaries.

The next department are your stakeholders. If this is a large corporation then the stakeholders are the shareholders. In a non-profit the stakeholders are the donors and or funding authorities and in smaller business the stakeholders may be the owner or partners of the owner. In most cases the key information shared in this example may be similar as what you would provide to the first department and consequently the information would have already been predetermined to assist you in what you report. However, this may also include less tangible information like feel good stories for the donors, information around larger projects that will take longer periods of time to accomplish for the shareholders, or customer feedback for the owners and/or partners of the owner.

The third department is your own. You need to be able to provide yourself with a snapshot on how your department is doing in achieving its own goals and objectives. The blue chips provide you with an immediate idea (snapshot) on how well your department is doing in achieving its objectives. An example might be employee retention rates, incident reporting, or sales targets.

The last department is the rest of the organisation. Your goal here is to collaborate key information across the entire organization for future improvements. The rest of the organization needs to have access to these blue chips in order to gain insight as to how the organization is doing as a whole. Some examples of blue chip information that the rest of the organisation needs to know about your department would be those items that would directly or indirectly impact those other departments. As an example if your department is responsible for delivery of a program / service then the information shared with other departments might be how busy or not that program / service is.

Let's unpack this a bit further with a few more examples:

The first example is your board, corporate head office, or the owner. They are responsible for the integrity, governance, vision, and financial management of the organisation. They carry an immense responsibility and consequently require blue chip information to help them make critical decisions on behalf of the organisation. The type of information they would require would be financial statements, sales forecasts, inventory reconciliation reports, and HR summary reports.

Therefore your blue chips would contribute to that information as much as your responsibilities allow you to contribute. If you are only in HR then your blue chips to this department might only be staff turnover rates, open positions and why they are open, and summary reports on yearly reviews as an example. However, if your department generates revenue then your blue chips would be reporting that revenue including information around sales forecasts and budgets.

The second example is your stakeholders. The stakeholders want to have information that supports the type of information that the first example has, except with this group they also want to understand the positive image of your organisation. If this is a small business they would want information that communicates positive customer reviews, increased customer counts, and repeat business. If this was corporate they would want information of community engagement and support, along with positive customer reviews and supporting information regarding high employee retention rates. For a non-profit the stakeholders (donors, funding partners) want to understand what positive work the organisation is doing in the community while clearly communicating the organisation's ongoing needs regarding the future success of the organisation's programs and services.

Once again depending on what department you are responsible for within your organisation you would tailor your blue chip reporting to reflect your area. If you were in HR this would involve a higher focus on those employee reviews and staff retention rates. This group would want to know stories around why it is a great place to work as an example. If you were in a department that generated revenue then stories around customer engagement / reviews would be the information they are looking for.

You are responsible for specific tasks and objectives as it relates to your specific department. This is reflected in your job description and was reflected through the training you received to do your job. In order to do that you need access to information as a way of determining how well you are doing in achieving those tasks and objectives. Think of it as a way of measuring your own success. As you focus on running your department well you need access to information from the rest of the organisation in order to help you gauge what running a department well even looks like.

The other departments in your organisation require access to your blue chip reporting in order to gauge how well they are doing in relation to the rest of the organisation. This information is used to better understand both the quality of your organisation's programming and services delivered as well as to understand emerging needs that you may need to change and adjust to in order to meet the objectives of the organisation as a whole. In other words, although practically speaking each department may operate somewhat independently of each other, the use of blue chip reporting helps make sure that everyone is working toward similar goals and objectives – and in a sense, staying on the same page.

Look over these four categories once again and examine the blue chips that would be associated with each category. Are there any blue-chip items that overlap or are duplicated? Eliminate the overlaps or duplications, combining them into one blue chip and then take a look at what is left. What you are left with will be a list of blue chips for you. You are responsible now for accurate reporting of those blue chips.

You are responsible to create systems of reporting and communicating within your department that will help you have immediate access to those blue chips. Ideally your supervisor or the Executive Director or the General Manager should be able to call you or walk into your office and ask for data on any of those blue chips and you will be able to immediately give them that information.

When you examine all four categories you get something like this:

- Financial statements
- Sales forecasts (or in a non-profit world revenue forecasts)
- Inventory control reports
- Positive customer reviews (or in a non-profit world positive stories from program/service participants)
- Increased customer counts (or in a non-profit world increased program usage)
- Employee retention rates
- Critical risk factors (emerging needs, barriers to growth, depreciating returns or funding sources ending)

When you take a look at your department or perhaps a better way of explaining it is to take a look at what you directly manage and have direct control over. A more succinct way of putting it is to measure your level of authority by determining what you can say 'yes' to. Then after that has been determined gather together these blue chips and build an effective method of communicating this information to the other three groups as requested.

So, from a practical standpoint if you have been given authority to generate financial statements make sure that they are at your fingertips, updated, and accurate. If you are directly responsible for customer interaction or in the world of a non-profit for program delivery then devise a system in which you can collect those positive reviews so they are available when asked for. This will take some reflection on your part but if you understand that you have a reporting responsibility to those three other groups that will help inform what you need to classify as blue chips within the scope of your job responsibilities.

To break this down even further if you are responsible to report on employee retention rates as a blue chip then you need to first build a system to capture that information. You could start by determining if any information is being collected around terminations or departures. Do you know how many people have left your organisation in the last month? Do you know how many people were hired in the last month? If not, find out and then build a system of reporting that captures that on an ongoing basis. These pieces of information will be the start of helping you report on employee retention rates.

Another example might be if you are responsible for some aspect of revenue for your organisation then make sure you have access to the sales forecast for your department. Do you know what the revenue expectations are for your department? How are you tracking your revenue right now? Once you combine those two pieces of information you are well on your way for blue chip reporting around sales revenue and forecasting.

This will take some time to work out and will require soliciting feedback from all of the key categories of your organisation. However, once you have identified what your blue chips should be and have become proficient at reporting on them you will find that your time is better managed, you are feeling less overwhelmed and overall a sense of being in control of your days. In other words you will have become a time management expert.

Coaching

When you hired that employee you did not hire a machine to do a task – you hired an individual in whom you expect will do much more than simply completely task work. Therefore, the expectation placed on you is that you will act as a coach from the very beginning of your employee's journey with your organisation. This expectation remains in place until the employee exits your organisation. Remember, this is the essence of the Exit Strategy – from recruitment through to termination and coaching is a very important part of that process.

A common complaint of a manager is this assumption that they thought their employees came pre-trained! There are some presuppositions that you tend to have as an employer concerning your employees. An example of some might be:

- Everything they put on their resume is the truth!
- The employee understands everything they put on their resume
- They fully learned how to do their last job with their last employer
- They cared about the job they had prior to applying with you
- They care about this job with you

In regards to training you need to think outside the box. As you continue to raise your standards you need to find ways to help your employees achieve those standards. This is part of your role as a manager to equip your employees with the tools they need to do their job. Keep in mind that you want to demonstrate that you are continually developing your people. Training your staff is the primary way that you as their employer can demonstrate that you are investing in your employees. If you don't train you don't care. It is as simple as that.

You have hired an employee and now you have to coach them. In particular it is important that there is a focus on coaching the employee for the duration of their probation period so you can make sure that they are a good fit for the organisation. This, of course, will minimize a whole host of problems that could come later and are addressed when I talk about progressive discipline later in the book.

As this new employee's immediate supervisor there is an expectation on you to document, coach, supervise, follow up, and to be intentional in absolutely everything to do with this new employee. Management is, after all, all about managing people and how you set up a new employee will play a large part in whether they will be successful or not. This includes the care during the interview, the thoroughness in the orientation, and the clear communication delivered when explaining policies and procedures. This does not just happen once but every time you communicate with an employee. If at any point during their probation period you find that they are not doing something correctly, then the very first item that you address is your communication.

Something important to remember as their manager is that you are not their friend! No matter how entwined your jobs become, or how close your job duties may overlap or come alongside your employee's you need to realize that the employee has entered into a contract with you as their employer. Thus, the relationship will always be an employer/employee. What this results in is a loneliness that can happen with the manager feeling very isolated and alone in their position of supervising staff. Thus, the reason for keeping contact with your peers – the other managers as a way to connect and have relationship outside of the ones you have with your staff.

Exercise:

Before I take the time to explain coaching here is an exercise to do at a staff meeting in order to gain an idea of how to put a team together.

Take two puzzles (smaller puzzles – normally under 30 pieces) and set them up on separate tables.

This is a race to see whose team can complete the task first.

Rules:

1. Divide into two teams
2. Choose positions
    a. Edge placer (the one who puts together the edge of the puzzle only)
    b. Flipper (the one who organizes all the pieces of the puzzle so the team can assemble it the fastest)
    c. Encourager (the one that participates in putting the puzzle together while cheering on their teammates)
    d. Leader (because every team needs a leader!)
3. As a point to step 2 lead each team in a discussion as to who is going to be each of the four positions. Then, once the leaders have been picked talk to both of them and give them the choice of either puzzle to do.
4. Get them to do the puzzles.

Debrief

1. Why did you choose the people you chose?
2. Did that strategy work for you?
3. Would you change the positions of the people if you had to do it again? Why or why not?
4. Leaders – what did you learn new about your team members through this exercise?

What is Coaching?

There are challenges to the work that you do as managers. Many times during your day, issues pop up, problems need to be solved, and challenges will stretch you. Your challenge is to develop your leadership abilities so that you are not creating chaos but minimizing and perhaps even preventing it throughout your organisation. Coaching plays an important part in this process, and each of you have a circle of influence in which you can be an effective coach, minimizing problems along the way.

Lots of people can become managers but very few managers can become leaders. When I talk about coaching I am referring to those managers who have worked hard at mastering their craft and are now considered leaders. If you ever want to test whether you feel you are a leader or not just look behind you and see who is following you. If there is anyone there – you are a leader. In this chapter my challenge to you leaders is to learn how to effectively coach your team and in that process develop other leaders.

There are a few checkboxes that will help you assess early in your days of learning on how to be an effective coach to see how you are doing. As an example coaches know their results are measured not by what happens when they're present, but by what happens when they're not present. If your team falls apart when you leave it is a sign of an ineffective coach. If you find yourself drained because you can't take a day off without some sort of crisis popping up, or your phone is ringing off the hook the challenge is not to look at your team for the reason why but to look at your coaching skills.

Coaches know it's not what they do that matters, but what their people do that matters. Being an effective leader and therefore an effective coach is never about your own glory or your own spotlight but instead it is about showcasing your team and helping them find success. A leader would know their own limits and realize the real power of an organization is when everyone is contributing and focused. A manager approaches this differently. They make success about them and they utilize antiquated motivational techniques based in fear and anger to get any sense of productivity out of their team. This may work in the short term but ultimately this approach will always end with the demise of the manager.

As a leader you stand alone as an example to your team. You become the common denominator that either unites your team or destroys it. This is even more so when you begin to actively engage your team as their coach. You need to know that you are being watched and measured, not just on what you do in public, but what you do in private as well. It's easy to do the right thing when everyone is watching, but coaches know what they do away from the front-line of their organization impacts how they act when they are on the front-line. They know other people are watching them in all scenarios. This is both the burden and responsibility of leadership. This is the cost but also the key to your success.

Your integrity is paramount and is your greatest asset as a leader who wants to effectively coach their team. Coaches don't talk about having integrity. They live it. The coach who talks about having integrity is the last person to have it. People who have integrity don't walk around telling others they have it. People know the coach has integrity because they see it in the coach's actions. Their integrity is what anchors them and allows others to believe and place value in them. Your integrity provides you with the invitation to speak into the lives of each person on your team and helps establish that coaching relationship so you can develop them into leaders. It always starts with you.

How To Communicate As A Coach

Coaching begins with a conversation, which occurs during the training of a new employee. Using the conversational style of interviewing you have already begun to make a connection with that new employee. This connection lays the initial foundation for successful coaching during the critical probation period. These conversations need to be productive and timely in order to help your new employee achieve their goals. Without a clear focus on goals, proper direction and the support from you to achieve them, your new employee is cast adrift in the rough seas of the workplace, left alone to navigate their way to success. It's the coach's responsibility to have the right conversations at the right time to help their people succeed. But what kind of conversations am I talking about?

The first type of conversation is called a calibrating conversation. All good coaching starts with clear goals and an agreement on how to achieve those goals. When coaching your new employee your initial conversations need to take more of a listening role. Why is the employee here? What are they hoping to accomplish? How will this job help them accomplish it? Out of those initial conversations will emerge some initial goals that you can begin to develop. Make sure the goal is relevant to the employee's job and is attainable with good effort. If those pieces are in place you can almost be assured the goal will be motivating to the individual.

Next, you have instructional conversations. These initial training focused conversations revolve around the functionality of their job ensuring that your new employee understands how to perform the basics of what is expected from them. This is done through demonstrating the skill, teaching the skill, and having your employee practice the skill. These instructional conversations with your new employee will build their competence and maintain their commitment and enthusiasm. Your employee needs you to explain the who, what, where, when, and why of the work they're being asked to do, as well as being given the necessary training and resources needed to accomplish their goals. Instructional conversations set a firm foundation for your employee's future success.

Then there are empowering conversations. Remember you did not hire a machine to do a task but an individual who brings their own enthusiasm rooted in their own goals and ambitions. However, sometimes your new employee will become discouraged with their lack of progress or success in achieving a goal. An empowering conversation blends high amounts of direction and support to pull your employee out of their disillusionment and help build their competence on the goal or task. This conversation will look like continued training, instruction, and assistance in problem solving. Your role would include listening, praise, and encouragement to help build your employee's commitment and motivation.

Each of these types of conversations need to be structured around a deliberate and planned one-on-one conversation. Initially it is recommended that these conversations occur weekly throughout the employee's probation period. They should roughly last between 15-30 minutes. Once your employee has successfully completed their probation period then your intentional coaching conversation should be planned for once a month thereafter as that helps you stay in touch with your employee's goals. Through those deliberate one-on-one conversations you provide your employee with the opportunity to ask for direction and any support they need from you. These one-on-ones keep the lines of communication open between coaches and employees and allow for mid-course corrections if their performance gets off-track.

If you are a manager striving to become a leader then like a coach you need to know how to play the game. To expect excellence from your team you must model excellence. A coach is not out playing the game, however if a coach does not know how to play the game that will quickly erode the coach's ability to lead their team. The expectation is that each of your employees will be watching you "walk the talk". In doing this you will model excellence to your team. The challenge here is for you to ask yourself – can you do the job that you expect each of your employees to do? If not, why not? You cannot coach someone effectively if you do not know how to do their job – and do it well.

If you want to be a coach answer these questions:

1. Do you know how to do the job that you are asking your employees to do?
2. Are you able to demonstrate excellence in the job that your employee is doing?
3. Are you consistent with your standards, applying them equally to yourself and your employees?
4. Do you make the tough calls early in the 'game'?
5. Are you lowering your standards out of desperation?
6. Have you been able to clearly establish the employer/employee relationship?

Reasons Why Managers Don't Fire Employees And Should

It is hard to make the 'tough call' at any point and unfortunately many managers shy away from doing so, lowering their standards out of desperation. A manager may have many reasons why they don't end an employee's employment but in the end if you want to become a leader and a strong coach for your team you need to rise above these reasons and make the tough call as early as possible in the game.

In my experience the biggest reason that managers have given me for not making the tough call earlier is that they see themselves as being 'too nice'. You need to understand that when someone is not performing, it is either because they are not motivated to perform or they do not have the skills. If you've tried a variety of motivational strategies and have offered skills training, and yet you still haven't seen significant progress, you and the employee are better off parting ways.

Firing may not seem "nice" in the short-term, but it's actually the kindest thing you can do for struggling employees in the long-term; the sooner they're fired, the sooner they can move on to jobs where they have a better chance to succeed. Don't let your self-image get in the way of doing what's right.

The second biggest reason for avoiding this unpleasant task is the realization that you will have to do their job while you find a replacement. Sometimes a replacement can't be found within the organization. Sometimes the only one suitable for doing the job is you, the leader. The search for a replacement may take a while, which makes it even harder for you to swallow the idea of doing your job and another one. Delaying firing is understandable, but not prudent.

You may feel like you have not given the employee enough time however, leaving a poorly performing employee in place not only delays the problem, it can amplify it. There is no telling how much of a drain this employee will place on morale and how much your leadership will be questioned—due to your tolerance of bad behavior or poor results.

Many managers have also struggled in making this type of call because the employee in question has been with the organization for a long time. Unfortunately, they have also been performing below minimal standards. If the deadline for improved performance has passed for this employee, start looking for a replacement. Don't keep restarting the clock because you are not going to get any better performance out of them. This may be a case of the employee wants to leave but doesn't know how to do so.

Loyalty is important to an organization's stability and sustainability. All the accumulated knowledge and wisdom held in your employees' minds helps you avoid past mistakes, maintain group identity, and support each other through ups and downs. Loyalty, though, is a two-way street. Is it loyal for an employee to decrease standards, disengage from those you work with, and remove accountability, or fail to develop new skills? Both parties need to have each other's' backs. Prolonged let-ups and let-downs are signs that the relationship has run its course.

Finally, managers often worry about the effect firing one employee will have on the rest of the team. The manager worries about being disliked. They worry about employees being angry or dispirited to the point where it decreases performance. The manager might worry about key employees protesting or leaving. Usually, though, if the fired employee was dragging the team down (and creating additional work for other employees), the team may miss the person, but they will celebrate your decision.

Manager versus Leader

I have been using the term 'manager' and 'leader' separately because as I have mentioned before there are many managers but very few leaders. I take this one step further by saying that only a leader can be an effective coach. If a manager attempts to be a coach they will end up destroying their team. There are reasons why I make this distinction between both terms and I want to take some time now to point out some distinctions.

A manager gives orders, coaches ask questions.

Shouting orders at your staff will turn them against you. Instead, ask your employees this: "What would you do?" or "What do you think of this idea?" By allowing your employees to participate in the decision-making process, you'll transform what could have been an order into something more easily swallowed. This type of questioning will also inspire creativity, motivation, and autonomy in your staff.

Managers criticize mistakes, coaches call attention to mistakes indirectly.

Pointing out your employees' mistakes directly will only leave them feeling embarrassed and frustrated. Effective coaches give their employees the chance to learn and grow letting them address their mistakes themselves.

Managers rarely praise, coaches reward even the smallest

improvement.

Praise is a must when it comes to effective coaching. Finding time to recognize your employees for even the smallest accomplishment will only increase their interest in what they do. Providing regular feedback and recognition is certain to show your employees you genuinely appreciate their efforts.

Managers focus on the bad, coaches emphasize the good.

This really comes down to seeing the cup half empty or half full. Only tuning into the flaws of a project or an employee doesn't leave room for learning or improvement. Build up the strengths and coach the weaknesses.

Managers want credit, coaches credit their teams.

Poor managers are always the first to take credit for positive praise; effective coaches understand the importance of crediting their team for the big wins. This pays off in the long run by establishing a more positive company culture where employees are driven toward more successes as a team. Management shouldn't be approaching through force, but rather through influence. Start improving your management style by injecting more coaching into it.

How To Be A Coach

What is a coach?

Have you ever watched a professional sports game like hockey, football or baseball? Let's look at these three coaches in three unique ways to help us better understand what it is that a coach does and find ways to apply these examples into our workplaces.

Let's start with the **Hockey** coach analogy.

This coach is all about knowing the strengths and weaknesses of each person on their team. Hockey boils down to this one factor for the coach. It is that the coach knows the strengths and weaknesses of each of his players. As a coach, it is critical to have a complete knowledge of each of your employees' strengths and weaknesses.

In understanding the limitations of each of these people you are able to make critical game decisions that will maximize the strength of each person and minimize their weaknesses. In order to best understand the strengths and weaknesses of our employees you need to understand the environment in which you expect them to work.

A work review process is taking a step out of your department and examining all the ways that your department is contacted externally, and how each of those contacts are processed within your department or internally. Another way of looking at this is a work process flow review. What this means is that for each position within your department (your position included) there are specific work tasks assigned to them.

You need to sit in the place of each position within your department and analysis all the work that comes to them, making sure that they have all the tools to efficiently and effectively finish that work. Repeating these steps for every work process in your department will quickly help you grow in your competence to do each position and also to set up a more effective department, ensuring that each of your employees have all the tools they need in order to complete every aspect of their job.

If your employees do not have all the tools to do their job you will be unable to assess their strengths and weaknesses accurately. At the end of this chapter I will take you through a basic work review process.

In hockey the coach may decide to change a couple of players on a line in order to bring a certain strength to each game. In your department, positioning your employees is critical to the success and effectiveness of the organisation. You may have an employee that is definitely not a people person but loves procedures and the established systems. This person may be better suited to be a support person in various capacities that would take them out of the direct interaction with the frontline.

You may have a very personable, very friendly employee that would be a tremendous asset in talking to each of these groups of people. Listen to the heart. Listen to understand, not with understanding. Take some time to sit down with each of your employees in order to hear their heart. Pay attention to their passions, interests, and fears. Observe them in different work and group settings so you can gain a sense of where they excel and where they struggle.

Are they strong in areas of conflict resolution or do they avoid conflict at all cost? Are they quite comfortable speaking to a group of people but are awkwardly silent when it is one on one?

These observations should be noted as you begin to discern where you should be placing and directing your people.

Let's understand action plans. The key to a successful action plan is to make it their idea. You can call these 'agreements', 'commitments', or 'action plans'. The timing of them is just as critical as the purpose of them. One appropriate time to utilize an action plan would be when you go through the employee review process. However, action plans should be used as a motivational tool from the employee to the employer with the employee making a commitment to the employer and consequently the employee holding the employer accountable for the implementation of the action plan goals.

The key to its success is that the action plan becomes the idea of the employee and is completed by the employee. Your feedback should only be in helping to steer the employee into areas that they need to be challenged on. There will be a tendency for the employee to develop an action plan that is very easy and does not require a lot of personal development in order to accomplish it so make sure you can pick up on those moments in order to challenge them into aspiring for something more challenging and consequently rewarding.

Your level of involvement in this exercise would be determined with how realistic the employee is being. At the end of the coaching process, you need your employee to walk away from it focusing on their strengths of their weaknesses and their weaknesses of their strengths. These attributes need to be included into their action plans. Remember that their action plans need to be measurable and timely. Take your time as you put together the action plan with your employee and remember you are building a foundation now for a successful business tomorrow!

The Exit Strategy informs us that not all employees are here because they are making a career out of this position. Therefore, your goal is to work with each employee to help them get all that they want out of this job in order to help set them up for success with whatever their next chapter of life may be. Consequently, you are invited to take a very active role in the development of each of your employees for however long you have them working for you.

By communicating your desire to work with each employee in order to help them be successful you are creating the ideal working atmosphere where the employee will be more open to examining their weaknesses and working toward a continuous improvement. The action plan is not a tool that is sprung on the employee but more a living document that you work towards with the employee leading the way.

Here is the action plan process. First is the hiring process, followed by the initial training and orientation. This is followed by the probation period, ongoing listening, ongoing coaching meetings and after one year their employee review. At this point the initialization of the action plan begins. As you take the time to listen and respond to their desires you can build an environment where you can create space for the employee to want to improve. As you bring the employee to a place where they are expressing those things that they would like to work on you can lead them to create their own action plan. Thus, throughout this process it has remained the employee's idea and that frees you up to be their coach, which will add a rich dynamic to the working relationship between the both of you.

Football

The next type of coaching analogy is football. The focus in this type of coaching is to empower key people to do key things (think quarterback). This type of coaching involves the ability to empower key people on your team to do their jobs with minimal involvement from you. This requires the skill to identify who those key individuals are (second in commands, lead shift supervisors) and to make sure they are equipped and trained to do their positions.

Football is a game which focuses on the completion of plays. A successful play in your work will be creating a positive customer experience. Depending on where the opponents' defense is, who they are, game conditions, how close you are to the goal line, and the ability of your players currently on the field will determine your next play. In other words, you, as the coach, need to determine where your team is at in any given moment, understanding and appreciating that your work environment is dynamic and faced with new challenges each day.

As the coach, you need to be able to read the signs of your players and determine when they need to have some time to recover during the game or if they can continue. However, the majority of responsibility is on your quarterback. The quarterback is out there in the thick of it. They have to make the tough calls and try to complete the plays in order to get that football to the goal line for a team touchdown.

In your organisation, you can apply this analogy this way: The quarterback is your team leader. The players are the employees that report to that team leader. The football is your customer and the goal line is a positive customer experience. Your opponents are the factors that would endanger that positive customer experience such as inconsistency, lack of care, lack of resources, and so on.

Now your role as the coach of this football game is to be able to assess all of these factors at once and determine whether your staff or the players are at optimum strength. You need to be able to identify possible factors that may spring up in an effort to thwart your opponent's attempts at a positive customer experience. This will require some practice and you may find that early in your attempts that you will make some bad calls. In doing your job correctly from the beginning you are able to give a strong tool to your team leader - thus empowering him/her to make the good decisions as well.

You are given various tools to help you do your part properly but if you aren't setting the example by following up with any issues then the tools will be inadequate when your team leaders go to use it. A lot of employee grumbling can originate in a frayed cord that has sat there for two months, no bandages in the first aid kit for the last week or the staff washroom that has grime build-up because so and so didn't do their job for the last few days.

Being a coach can be difficult but trying to be the coach and the players at the same time is impossible.

By making sure you do your part properly and thoroughly will enable your team leaders and ultimately your employees to do their job properly and thoroughly. Remember what I have talked about in regards to trust and good communication. Without both of those being used and practiced you will never succeed in creating a successful department.

Baseball

The last type of coaching analogy is baseball. The goal with the baseball coach is in understanding your own language (think of all the symbols and gestures that the various coaches and players use). This type of coaching requires the ability to communicate efficiently and effectively with every member of your team with a language that they all understand and can respond to immediately.

As is common within most organizational systems there is a language with embedded meaning that is known only to those within the organization. As a coach you need to be aware of this language and teach this language to your employees in order to create the foundation for effective communication. Communication is critically important. If your employees have no idea on the direction you are going or what is happening around them – or with each other – then there is a breakdown.

In baseball there is the coach in the dugout and there is a coach at each base for the players. Baseball is a game of constant changing strategy, planning ahead several innings at a time and interconnectedness between everyone on the team. Every player in every position has a very critical role to play in such that if the short stop is out of position there may be an opportunity missed to get a double play (two out). Everyone needs everyone in a baseball game.

In your department you can start to apply this analogy this way: the coach in the dugout is you. The coaches on the bases are your team leaders. The players would be your employees. Now initially if you don't have enough team leaders on your team then one of those bases won't be covered which could create a weakness if the player is unsure how to react to a play.

In each department one of the very first areas that you need to focus on developing is your team leader. A good measuring stick to determine if you have enough team leaders or not is to answer this question. If you weren't scheduled at all for one week in your department, do you have enough team leaders to take care of any issues for that week? If you come back after a week off and there are issues in your department then you have holes in your department. There will be times that an area in your department will be weak and bad decisions could be made by inexperienced employees not ready to handle that level of responsibility.

A critical element in baseball is the communication between the players and the coaches. I am amazed when I watch and I see all these gestures and hand motions that are recognized by the other players and acknowledged simply by a nod. Within your department this must be something that you strive for. If the players don't understand clearly what the coach is asking (the manager) then you cannot expect your employees to follow through with your instructions. You all need to be on the same page.

So, if as the coach you have laid out certain expectations then you need to have your employees understand not only what that is talking about or how they would go about achieving that goal but also why they are doing it in the first place.

Your Goal

Your goal in coaching is to win. To win in your context is to deliver a positive experience to every customer you have contact with.

You cannot do it all.

Never.

As a coach the best measure of success you can achieve is to see your employees succeed. You have a unique place of importance in their lives. You have been granted a place of privilege, to influence, to encourage, to develop, to equip, and to help launch them into greater things. It is all about them. The employees. It is not about you.

If you are not actively developing that next leader, then what are you doing? Because it isn't coaching.

I should be able to ask you to identify at least one person in your department who you think has the 'right stuff' and could potentially do your job. This is your goal. This is your responsibility. This is your measure of success. If you are not developing your people than you are not doing your job. It is that simple.

In summary you need to remember weekly coaching meetings for new employees, which means 15 minutes of intentional conversations. This is critical to laying a solid foundation for a new employee. Without this the chances of developing an excellent employee will be greatly diminished. These weekly coaching sessions need to be a top priority for you – their manager.

Monthly coaching meetings for ongoing employees are necessary. These are 15 minutes of intentional conversations and this is on top of a monthly department staff meeting. Once you have coached an employee successfully through the three-month probation period you need to continue to demonstrate your desire to invest in them. The one-on-one contact with your employees helps instill loyalty, connection, affirmation, and acceptance – all critical elements to fostering an amazing work environment for your employees.

Additional coaching may be required for projects and leadership development. This is done as needed, when needed, and as long as needed.

As you move forward with individual leadership development with one or more of your employees you have to raise your level of intentional time commitment to them in order to help them become successful in their new skills. This is akin to teaching a child how to ride a bike. You want them to be successful so take the initial time to make sure they really understand how to do these new tasks before setting them off on their own.

The expectation is that you will utilize all three coaching methods as needed in the development of your team. You will identify and develop those key employees sooner rather than later and you will recognize the embedded language in your department and make sure you practice clear communication at all times with your employees.

Establishing Commitments

Answer this question; five frogs are sitting on a log. Four decide to jump off. How many are left?

Five, because deciding is different than doing. Decisions are worthless unless you turn them into commitments[ix].

In the 1980s through to the early 1990s the predominate managerial approach was a power over stance. The employee simply did what they were told because they wanted to keep their job. Working under the threat of losing one's job was – or seemed to be enough of a motivation for the employee. However, in North America as the economy began to shift and the baby boomers got a bit older there emerged a new generation of employees who began walking away from these types of managers. I know because I was one of those managers whose employees began to walk away from.

New management methods were needed in order to retain good staff and another thousand books on management were published, all with similar themes. It was time to listen to the employee and when the retail / service industry did listen they found new ways to motivate their employees. I read the newest books and I took the courses and attended the workshop as I still wanted to be a successful manager in this new age of management.

But it still wasn't enough as the employees were staying in their roles for shorter amounts of time (six months was considered tenure now) and their productivity was at an all-time low. Enter psychology. Coaching and goal creating needed to be something that the employee did – they needed to feel like it was their decision and their plan from the start. As managers if we could not only get our employees to buy into the corporate plan but to lead them to a place where the employee made it their plan – their goal - then all of a sudden the employee's productivity shot up. Like all management methodologies this was not without its flaws and like psychology this particular approach has evolved over the years.

Now there is a greater understanding of how people think and with the Exit Strategy since our approach is based on communicating worth and value to the person – recognizing their individuality in the process there is value in also understanding how people enter into commitments. You want to make a supporter out of the employee right from recruitment through to their departure. You want to invest in that employee every step of the way but like in anything without a commitment the employee will falter and you as their manager will become frustrated with them.

Therefore it is important to understand how commitments work. In a professional conversation, your employee's decision states their intention, but a commitment holds them accountable. Although a commitment does not guarantee that the employee will follow through, it's far more reliable than a decision. More importantly, when managed properly, it allows you to handle breakdowns with effectiveness, trust and integrity.

Have you been in meetings where lots of decisions are made but nothing gets done and nobody is held accountable? Unless you finish the meeting with commitments about "who will do what by when," you've just built 90% of a bridge. You can move your team forward but as they approach the end of this unfinished bridge the frustration on everyone's part spills over, which will damage relationships and culture. A lack of commitment will bring about inefficiencies, mistrust, and corruption. To avoid this erosion of your team you need to incorporate commitments into every deliberate coaching conversation you have with your employees.

The typical way to avoid making a clear request is to make a muddled one. Do you recognize any of these examples?

It would be great it…

Someone should…

Do we all agree to…?

Can you try to…?

The boss wants…

To establish a commitment from your employee you must speak it in the first person, using direct language. You must be clear on the conditions of the commitment, including time. Although there are many ways to establish a commitment, the most effective ones follow a common pattern:

In order to get A (a want or need), I ask that you deliver B by C. Can you commit to that? This simple formula contains three key elements. (A) refers to a clear and articulated need or want. A bad example might be, "I need to know how many of our products and/or services were used in the last six months." A good example might be, "I need to know how many new customers used this specific product and/or service in the last six months."

The second element (B) refers to the method or delivery of the request. Are you asking for an email summary? An excel report? A Google Drive document? Be specific with how (A) is presented to you.

The last element (C) refers to time. Make sure that your requests are always followed with a time element in order to help the employee gauge the level of urgency with the request. By asking the question – can you commit to that – you are requiring the employee to read through the request and assess whether or not the request is both manageable in terms of time and method and is achievable in terms of timeline. With their yes response you both now have a way of keeping each other accountable.

Let's expand the question: Can you commit to that? A well-formed request demands a clear response. There are only three possible answers to your question around commitment:

Yes, I commit.

No, I decline.

I can't commit yet because I need clarification, I need to check; I promise to respond by X, I want to propose an alternative, I can make it only if I get Y by Z.

Here are some interesting ways by which employees often say, "No, I don't commit."

Yes, I'll try.

Okay, let me see what I can do.

Seems doable.

Let me check into it.

Someone will take care of it.

When the employee declares, "I commit," they assume the responsibility to honor their word unconditionally. They take on an obligation to deliver on their promise; or if they can't, to do their best to take care of the requestor. When they declare, "I decline," they might still try to do what they were asked, but they don't commit. They do not give the requestor the right to hold them accountable. It is much better to have a clear "no" than to get bogged down in a wishy-washy "I'll do my best."

There are many good reasons to decline. They may not have the resources; they may not have the skills; they may have a conflict with a previous commitment; they may anticipate problems; or they may just not want to do it. In order to make coaching as successful as it can be commitments play an important part of the coaching conversation. Poorly worded commitments that really are not commitments at all will eventually erode your ability to effectively coach any employee. Conversely, if you are unable to get clear commitments from your employees your ability to coach them will also be ultimately undermined by wishy-washy timelines and a lack of accountability.

How To Do A Work Process Flow Review

The purpose of a work process flow review is to take yourself out of your office and to put yourself into the shoes of each of your employees. The intent or outcome is to clearly establish where there are a duplication of tasks or services, whether your employees clearly understand what to do with every interaction that comes their way and whether they have the resources or training to handle the work.

To begin let's start with your position. On a blank piece of paper write down the left-hand side all the various ways that you are contacted. This could be phone calls, emails, mail, or in-person. For some processes – like phone calls – it can remain relatively simple in the beginning of this exercise. However, when you look at 'in-person' as an example you immediately need to understand more of the processes and purposes of your department before you can identify the next steps. As an example some in-person contacts might be employees asking you for help with their own tasks – to trouble shoot some aspect of their job duties. However, part of your organizational structure includes a supervisor where it is clear that your employees are to go to your supervisor first with those types of requests. What you have identified here is a breakdown in the work flow process and it provides you with a place to start investigating why.

What is helpful here is to identify what is currently happening and make adjustments afterwards, instead of trying to create an ideal picture through this exercise. If your in-person contacts involve staff asking misc. questions than let that be one option for the next box. If another in-person contact is another manager who has a question than make that a second option for the second box. If another in-person contact is a customer than make that the third option for the second box. Keep going until you have listed all the common in-person contacts that you have.

Once you have listed all the options go back to the list and write in the next step. As an example, if your first option for in-person contacts was your staff asking miscellaneous questions than write down the summary information/tools that you need in order to address those questions. Repeat this for the rest of the options on your list. What will emerge in this process – especially when you add in the process flows for your employees will be the following:

1. You will begin to see some possible duplication of work processes being done by you and your employee or by your employees in general.

2. You will begin to see where multiple points of initial contacts made to you or your employees are seeking similar types of information, thus leading you to develop a universal tool in order to effectively communicate that information to larger amounts of people (such as Google Docs/Calendar/mass emails, etc.).

3. You will begin to identify areas of your own job that could be easily transferred to an employee – thus improving your own work flow processes and empowering your employees to be more effective in their own positions.

4. You will identify areas of coaching opportunities that you can

implement with your employees in order to create a better experience for the customers that would come in contact with your department.

Ultimately, as the manager, you are responsible for every aspect of your department. In the next chapter I will talk about the three reasons why people fail: They Don't Know, They Can't Do, or They Don't Care. If you think about these three reasons as pointing a finger at someone please note that there are three fingers pointed back at you. In other words, if an employee fails, two out of those three reasons is because of you – their manager. Things like a work process review are only examples of tools that a good manager – a coach turned leader would use in order to best set up their employee for success. From recruitment through to termination – if you are not at every step of the way helping set up your employee for success then what is it that you are doing?

Progressive Discipline

Oh Oh! My Employee Did Something Bad. Now What?

Have you ever quit a job?

Have you ever been fired by a job?

How did your employer fire you?

The objective of the Exit Strategy is that the termination of the employee's employment should never be a surprise to you and especially to the employee. In my experience, over 80% of all employees that I have had to fire wanted to be fired. For a variety of reasons, they could not bring themselves to a place of quitting and so all that I was doing was drawing out the obvious. In a handful of cases, I have had the employee thank me for firing them – sometimes up to a couple years later. This is why I no longer refer to firing as termination but instead I call it helping someone leave.

This is certainly a weird aspect of human organizational behavior but one that I have observed over and over these past 25 years. Thus, I can say with a very high level of confidence that it should be of absolutely no surprise to the employee when their employment is terminated. If it is, you have done something seriously wrong along the way. In addition, it is also possible to communicate worth and value to an exiting employee – one whom you have had to terminate. It is possible to still have a 'supporter' of the organisation when they exit from you. Just because they have left employment with you, does not necessarily mean that your relationship to them has ended – it has simply changed.

Nobody enjoys disciplining an employee, except perhaps a total narcissistic dictator styled manager and if that is the case for you – perhaps you are reading the wrong book. Disciplining is difficult because most of the time it is wrought with conflict, heated emotions, and littered with conjectures. Most likely you have been brought into the situation because another employee has had enough of the antics of the offending one and like small children on the playground they do not know how to handle their petty differences so they drag in the 'grown-up'.

With a heavy sigh you get up from your sanctuary called an office, way at the back of the building – just off of the stock room and you follow this overly excited employee out to the front to 'deal with it'. You are aware that this employee that is requiring some form of discipline has been a pain in your ass for a while and so far has not responded to any of your 'interactions' with them. Feeling frustrated yourself you approach this employee, standing around talking to their friends, and you begin to yell at them.

"Get your lazy ass back to work!", you begin slowly working up to a feverish pitch, "OR YOU'RE FIRED!" You storm off back to your office – feeling pretty good about the level of authority you just exerted back there – not noticing that this same employee was giving you the middle finger as you walked away.

Perhaps you are not familiar with progressive discipline. It is an important managing skill to learn as it has its roots in labour law everywhere. Simply stated progressive discipline represents the corrective steps put in place in an effort to help an employee become successful at their job – regardless of how much you may dislike their personality or work ethic. It involves coaching, verbal warning, written warning and then either suspension or termination – depending on the factors involved. The key here is documentation – writing everything down. Recording every conversation you have with an employee as that serves as part of the record for progressive discipline.

When documenting discipline, you need to accomplish two things. First is to be specific about what the employee did wrong. Was the employee late multiple times? List them. Did the employee not follow procedures around intake or did the employee vary from regular programming? List them. List each incident. Give detail.

Second is to relate that specific item back to a larger theme. A larger theme is examining an underlying motivation or attitude that may be influencing the employee's behavior. An employee who is late all the time may be exhibiting a don't care attitude that may begin with being late but may spill over into other areas of their performance. When you record this for the employee you use reflective language such as, it would seem that being at least 10-15 minutes late your last 4 out of 7 shifts is demonstrating a don't care attitude and I am concerned that this attitude will impact your overall work performance.

The reason for the larger theme is twofold. First is that it helps lay the foundation for future progressive steps if necessary. Laying the foundation is very important. You are trying to rectify an employee's behavior, which is impacting their ability to do their job to the level of performance that you need them to be at. Therefore, that larger theme piece becomes a point of conversation that you can easily go back to in future progressive disciplinary conversations.

An example might be that the employee who was late several times is now more or less showing up on time but is not completing their reports or are sending them in not completed. Because you addressed the larger theme in the first step of progressive discipline you can now progress to the second step, highlighting the larger theme as the main reason for escalating the progressive discipline. If you do not include this larger theme then you simply have two first step disciplinary measures – one for being late and the other for not completing reports. They are, of course, related but if you do not do the work of laying the foundation and drawing out potential behavioral issues the first time then you miss your opportunity to deal with in consequent disciplinary conversations.

Second is that it helps protect the organization by using language more commonly accepted by the labour board, and courts of law. As progressive discipline is supervised by HR, they will help you with thematic language commonly used and accepted with the labour board. Language like insubordinate behavior is an accepted reason for termination with the labour board but difficult to prove in a wrongful dismissal case where you have not properly drawn that out throughout the disciplinary steps.

In laying the foundation you need to keep in mind that you must always address behavior and any underlying attitudes. There is normally a reason why an employee did something incorrectly whether that be procedural or policy-related. It is important to understand that reason instead of just focusing on the task, which was done incorrectly. This will help minimize future conflict as well as address any secondary reasons that may go missed such as inadequate supervision, tools, or improper training.

Addressing the behavior is not a way of attacking the employee or 'looking for something wrong' but is an exploratory and often quite effective method in which to address underlying circumstances that are impacting the employee's ability to do their job. Often in these coaching conversations where the manager reflects what they see as a bad behavior, the employee has enough space in the conversation to express what might be a motivating reason behind what has been interpreted as a bad behavior.

In the example of an employee being late continuously it is possible in this type of conversation that the employee will open up and share that they are going through a separation or they have some other crisis in their personal life that is quite a distraction. Although that won't stop the progressive disciplinary process it will help inform it and perhaps now there are some resources that you as their manager and with help from HR can offer the employee to assist them. When you miss this step, you miss a very important opportunity to care for your employees.

The best practice is when you meet with an employee, summarize the conversation with the employee in an email, send a copy to the employee and copy it to your supervisor. This improves accountability both ways along with transparency and helps establish a paper trail for later on.

Here is a simple philosophy to help keep all of this in perspective. There are three reasons why people fail. The first is that they don't know, the second, they can't do, and the third is that they don't care.

The first reason why an employee may fail is that they don't know. If that is the case then the first place you need to look is at yourself. Have you trained them completely – or at least to the exact same level as you have trained everyone else who is doing the same job. Have you provided them with the means, opportunity to access helpful resources in case they have forgotten?

The second reason why an employee may fail is that they can't do. Again, you need to look at yourself as their manager and employer. One example of this might be not listening to the employee's needs in terms of availability and now they are in a place where they are saying no to shifts you are scheduling them for. Another example might be their inability to complete the responsibilities of the job. Through coaching conversations, you may identify that the employee is really struggling with personal situations and they are struggling to know what to do with that.

In addition, it could be that an employee simply cannot do the job for some other reasons. Have you improperly placed them into a position in your organization and do you need to consider moving them into another area of your organization? It could be that an employee thought they would enjoy working in one department, however they found that they couldn't do it and perhaps they would be a better fit in another department.

The third reason that people fail is that they don't care. The harsh message with this type of person is that there is nothing you can do to change that. If they don't care – they need to leave. You cannot try to fix this or motivate the employee so do not try. Sometimes you can explore this with the employee by asking direct reflective questions like, "Your actions here seem to be showing a don't care attitude and I am concerned about that". This opens up immediate space for the employee to say no and offer some more insight to their particular behavior or it creates space for them to self-assess and make that determination that perhaps that is true – they don't care and if so then perhaps it is time that they moved on and left their employment with you.

Keep these three reasons in mind with every intentional conversation you have with your employees. I have taught that if you clearly identify that an employee has a don't care attitude then there is absolutely nothing you can do but to help that employee leave – chances are they want to leave anyway but need you to help them. It is far more difficult to fix the first two and the solutions can only come out of clear and consistent coaching conversations. It is possible that you may need to help an employee leave who is unable to overcome the first two reasons but not without a lot of help on your end to help them find success within your organisation.

Remember, just because their resume may have said that they have the skills and knowledge to do the job doesn't actually mean that they do – only that they have worked somewhere that there was an expectation that they had those same skills and knowledge. And if they did not receive the training in their previous employment then it is up to you to either train them or to find them unsuitable for the position and therefore need to help them leave. Your employees do not necessarily come pre-trained!

Remember, most of your employees are only here for a season and so be intentional about developing them. Why? Because it looks good on their resume. You want the employee to put your organisation on their resume. You want the employee to talk about your organisation as a past job. It is potentially good advertising for you – if you have done your job well.

The next reason to help an employee leave well is that it reflects on you as an employer. People talk. And you want them to talk. Hopefully you have done your job well so you will have ex-employees share with their friends, family and their next group of fellow employees how well a job you did in training them, providing work experience, and providing an amazing work environment for them.

Lastly, it keeps a partner and supporter going forward. If your organisation is a business, perhaps this means that they will return as a customer. If your organisation is a non-profit then as they speak well of your organisation perhaps that means that they or someone they talk to would become a supporter of your non-profit. Either way it benefits you if you can possibly keep them as a supporter when they leave their employment with you.

In summary there are two sides of the coin when it comes to the Exit Strategy. The first side is to hire knowing what you need to know in case you have to fire. Basically, this refers to the need to document everything and to make sure that every conversation you have with your employees are intentional conversations. This means that when you offer the commitment to ongoing coaching when you hire them that you follow through with your commitment to them.

The flip of this is to hire with the intention to develop, train, and equip the employee to succeed in their job. Everything you do with the employee needs to be intentional. You did not hire an employee to do a task. You hired an employee to create an opportunity for them to contribute to your organization in a mutually beneficial way. That requires very real effort on your part. It demands an intentionality to purposely train, develop, and equip the employee to succeed. You want them to succeed. This is your mandate as a manager. This is your purpose.

The other side to this coin is to fire knowing that you have done everything you could since you hired the employee. Keep in mind the three reasons why people fail. Make sure that in each case you have taken a long look at the first two reasons in order to be sure that you have done all that you could.

The flip of this is to fire with the intention to develop, train, and equip yourself to be successful in your job. When an employee exits your organization, the learning does not end with their departure but instead is shifted to yourself where you can be reflective, you can see what areas need to be tightened up, what new resources need to be developed, what areas you were weak in, all so you can strive to collectively become a better and better organization to be connected with. This is the Exit Strategy. Follow this strategy and you will develop leaders and partners while contributing to the overall success of the organization.

How To Confront In A Productive Way

In the workplace unproductive confrontation usually begins due to lack of information, misunderstanding, stressful working conditions, unresolved conflicts, personality differences, and power structures within the organization[x]. The irony is that because of these various elements present in the workplace there exists the need for confrontation. The intent behind the need for confrontation is to introduce the space to have intentional conversations where the end result is to element these various factors. The problem is that there exists the tendency to minimize these factors instead of having a constructive confrontational conversation where you could find a way to eliminate the factor all together instead of settling on minimizing.

Much of the negativity about confrontation stems from a limited view that confrontation is nothing more than a mixture of conflict and anger. However, confrontation is nothing more than an intentional conversation and those types of conversations are by far the best way to communicate worth and value to your employee. These types of conversations also help equalize various relationships within your organisation and that in of itself invites collaboration instead of conflict.

By avoiding the intentional conversation you may indirectly provoke accusatory and negative behaviors in the workplace, reducing them to a place of high stress, inefficiency and high absenteeism. By separating out the conflict from confrontation and focusing on the intentional conversation you can foster healthy and productive communication not just between you and your employees but you will be modeling how to have better conversations between the employees themselves.

Negative confrontation takes place when people discussing an issue lose sight of the organisation's goal and vision. Condescending and irrational talk, based on personal likes and dislikes make the discussion unprofessional. This should serve as a pause for each of you to reflect on where you are at. If any of you have lost sight of the organisation's goal and vision then perhaps you can find yourself falling into a place of negative confrontation.

In an intentional conversation, people might disagree and get overly passionate and assertive, but at no point does the discussion become personal or unprofessional. This is an invitation for you to practice healthy boundaries and to maintain the employer/employee relationship. Without those structures and boundaries in place, your ability to properly manage your people will soon erode to a place of negativity and conflict.

Initially, most of the intentional conversations will occur within your coaching conversations and then perhaps in those progressive disciplinary meetings. Over time, you will begin to use intentional conversations techniques in all of your conversations, inviting collaboration from the person you are having the conversation with. Ideally, done well, intentional conversations will lead to better employee retention and overall enjoyment in the workplace.

Myths Of Confrontation

Before I unpack how to have an intentional conversation – let's first take a look at some myths surrounding confrontation in the business place[xi].

Myth #1: Confrontation is negative.

Confrontation means to face something or someone head on, directly, and purposefully. Confronting something or someone is an attempt to forge a solution, seek a remedy, or simply stay on top of a situation. When negativity becomes part of the confrontation, collaboration is lost and you will not be able to gain a commitment from your employee.

Myth #2: Confrontation can be avoided.

Confrontation is inevitable. It is up to you to decide if it will be constructive or destructive. If important issues and expectations aren't confronted sooner, in a positive way, they'll need to be confronted later, when everything is negative. People are generally wired to avoid confrontation most of the time mistaking confrontation with conflict.

The problem with this strategy in the workplace is because of the very hierarchical structure of an employer and an employee there will inevitably be important issues and expectations that will need to be confronted. To avoid confrontation will ultimately lead to your demise as an effective manager.

Myth #3: There is nothing constructive about confrontation.

When confrontation is used as part of a deliberate, intentional, and systematic approach to organizational productivity, it is constructive.

Confronting issues that both parties agreed to address on a predetermined and consistent schedule is a powerful tool for replacing confusion with clarity, which helps everyone feel better.

This is why I suggest having weekly coaching during the initial probation period of a new employee. During those initial weeks of a new employment are the perfect opportunities for you as the new employee's manager to practice healthy confrontation conversations in the effort to bring about a strong commitment from your new employee. If done well during the probation period it will make future conversations that much easier while initially setting up your new employee for success because clear instructions have been laid as a solid foundation to the employee's continued employment.

Myth #4: Continuously confronting progress is micromanaging.

There exists this idea that generally speaking employees tend to push back and resent their work being monitored. However, lack of clear direction and consistent leadership involvement draw the loudest complaints. People work better when management takes an active interest in what they're doing. Resentment is a direct result of unfulfilled expectations.

How To Have An Intentional Conversation

Intentional conversations increase accountability on both the manager and the employee while decreasing potential conflict. When things are not confronted early and often in an intentional way they tend to crash and burn. By then, there is nothing left but conflictual, accusatory, negative, blame-placing, find-a-scapegoat, search-for-the-guilty-and-punish-the-innocent confrontation.

No thanks.

Avoidance will always lead to the demise of the manager before the demise of the employee. Intentional conversations are the strongest tools available to ensure effective leadership across an entire organization, at every level. The construction of an intentional conversation, with its confrontation, commitment, and celebration, keeps accountability high and conflict low by eliminating confusion, chaos, inconsistent messages, and double standards.

These are three parts of an intentional conversation.

The first part is confrontation. This is the act of confronting the action itself – or the problem - in an externalizing way. As a way of remembering this think of the idea of the person is not the problem – the problem is the problem. You as the employee's manager are addressing the problem of poor performance. Keep that idea separate from the person or else you will not be able to continue to communicate worth and value through this process and the likelihood of it resulting in a conflict is quite high.

Remember the three reasons why someone fails. In confronting the problem of poor performance you are inviting the employee to explore those three reasons – Don't Know, Can't Do, or Doesn't Care. Ideally, you will discover some reasons around the first two that will help lead this conversation into the next stage of an intentional conversation – that being commitment.

The second part is commitment. Right from recruitment you have begun this journey with your employee where your focus as their manager – or as their coach – is to help them succeed. However, in order to help them succeed they need to provide you with a commitment. Those individual commitments – or goals that come out of every single intentional conversation will all feed to the larger goal that the employee is working toward. Remember every conversation you have with your employee needs to end with them having made a solid commitment to you and more importantly to themselves or else conflict has space to enter into the employee/employer relationship.

As the manager you would discuss specific goals with the employee, the schedule for reaching the goals, and the process for achievement. This aspect of the intentional conversation becomes a negative and potentially frightening proposition when it is not engaged early enough. This is why it is important to have established weekly coaching meetings with every new employee for their probation period and then monthly afterwards.

The last part is celebration. Rewarded behavior is repeated behavior. Celebration helps keep the intentional conversation productive. Just as success over time builds confidence, appropriate recognition for every level of effort builds goodwill and the desire to meet and exceed expectations the next time.

In order to understand how this approach works let's consider the following situation at the office. An employee consistently deflects, resists, or lashes back each time you initiate an open an honest discussion of an issue. You've become frustrated or upset with this person's attitude and inability to hear your message. You'd like to express how it is for you, get to an understanding or agreement, and move on. Have you thought about why they would be resisting? Just to be difficult? Fear? Self-preservation? If the other person's behavior is bothering you then you own the decision about how to handle it. Your options are: avoid, accommodate, defer to someone else, or confront.

Don't expect the other person to notice you are bothered. If you tend to avoid confrontations, an important question to ask yourself is "Will the situation change if I do nothing?" If you confront, you might arrive at a win-win (negotiated) solution, a compromise, or no deal. In the overall strategy of managing employees the utilization of the intentional conversation is a given. It is a must.

From the point of recruitment where you are utilizing the skills of conversational interviewing you are also having an intentional conversation. You are determining if this candidate would make a great employee for the organisation. Even in that initial conversation

– if done well, you are employing the three main sections of an productive conversation: commitment, confrontation, and celebration. You are confronting them with aspects of their resume in order to potentially identify any conflicts. You are searching for a commitment from this candidate and potentially you are celebrating with them as you offer them the job!

It doesn't stop there though. Their probation period is the next period of time where the intentional conversation serves you well. You have to make a determination as to whether they will be a good long term fit for the organisation so here again we can see the three parts of the intentional conversation. You are meeting and coaching the employee weekly – confronting them with aspects that you need them to address. Through that process you are continually leading the employee to make a long-term commitment to their job and at the end of the employee's probation period you can then celebrate with them.

Finally, a key aspect to The Exit Strategy is the idea that you never terminate an employee but simply help them leave. In using the intentional conversation throughout their employment even progressive discipline can be done through the intentional conversation and when it comes time to part ways both you and the employee can see it coming, thus eliminating any conflict at that point. I have even experienced those conversations as being celebratory because as I have mentioned earlier it has been my experience that 80% of those I have terminated wanted to be fired as they couldn't bring themselves to quit. Intentional conversations make that process a lot smoother and with much less conflict.

Assertiveness

Assertiveness is a critical skill that you will need as a manager. You will need this skill in dealing with your employees and the customers. Without it, you lack professionalism, you lack leadership, and you will introduce chaos into your organisation. You may not know how to make decisions. You may not know how to effectively lead your team. You may not know how to get your team to follow you. You need to learn how to make decisions – effective and knowledgeable decisions. You need to learn how to lead and what to do in order to have your team follow you. This takes assertiveness.

Your assertiveness is born out of your self-confidence and assurance in the gifts and talents that you have. However, sometimes your confidence can take a beating in life or through the workplace and consequently your ability to be assertive will diminish. This most likely will not happen all of a sudden but gradually, over time. There are signs that you can look for – to identify whether your ability to lead and to maintain a strong leadership has diminished.

An early trap with inexperienced managers is to focus on a favorite employee. This most likely came about because this employee affirmed your leadership, they stroked your ego, and even perhaps got things done, making you look good in the process. It is an easy place to go – favoring employees – but by doing this it will impact your decisions in hiring, firing, promotion, discipline, and project assignments.

Perhaps you are taking things too personally. When things are bad, unintended emotions, stress, or reactions might surface. Managers with low-levels of confidence will personalize these outbursts or temporary states of behavior and allow it to impact beliefs, long-term perceptions, and relationships in the future. Taking things personally is only appropriate when things are personal. An employee's stressed out reaction to a bit of feedback from you, for example, is usually not about you, but the employee's concern about the meaning of the feedback. Don't get caught up in these spirals as it very quickly will undo your assertiveness and consequent ability to lead your team.

Are you getting defensive? If an employee asks a question and you interpret the seeking of additional information as a questioning of judgment and you then react as if that were fact, your confidence is an issue. If you want to be an effective leader you need to possess a level of confidence that shields against concern over what others think when asking "why".

Pay attention to fear. If you feel fearful of the unknown then this is another way of recognizing that your assertiveness has diminished. New managers in particular often feel as if they must know everything in order to lead well. If this feeling persists, and no contrary guidance is provided, the first time something comes up that they do not know, they may fear looking foolish. That fear will turn into covering up, making stuff up, and generally mucking up an organization.

How can you be assertive? There is a list of qualities and skills that will help you become more confident, more assertive in a professional way – in a way that will help you become a leader and become someone that people will want to follow.[xii] The first quality will always be integrity. You need to always do the right thing regardless of sentiment, and never compromise your core values. If you cannot build trust and instill confidence with your employees through your integrity you will not succeed as a manager.

People of integrity don't say one thing and do another. They don't talk negatively about members of their team behind their backs. They don't blur ethical boundaries when it comes to how they handle their money, their family, or their workweek. They are exactly who they present themselves to be. Don't be fooled – your people are watching you and they are evaluating you.

Is this person someone I can trust?

Will they keep their word?

Will they have my back when they say they will?

When the answer to those questions is YES, your employees will respect you as a leader.

You need to learn how to leverage experience. Inexperience, a lack of maturity, needing to be the center of attention, not recognizing limitations, a lack of judgment, an inferior knowledge base, or any number of other common mistakes made by rookie managers can cause your house of cards to fall. If you don't have the experience personally, hire it, contract it, but by all means acquire it.

You need to possess a strong presence and bearing. These leaders are strong individuals that never let you see them sweat. Everything about how they carry themselves messages that they have a clear vision and are capable of leading in accordance with said vision. Assertiveness promotes self-confidence not arrogance and when people around you feel as if you know what you are doing it speaks to your competence and consequently their safety.

When dealing with a difficult customer then your assertiveness first looks like competence. They need to know that you know what to do next – even if they don't want to immediately listen – they need to know that you are confident in this circumstance. In that place you can begin to de-escalate the situation as required, relying on your personal self-confidence and solid grasp of the situation to guide both you and who you are speaking with. Remember, what people want most in a conflict situation is someone outside of themselves to take charge and administer 'justice'. Your very presence and body language needs to reflect your high level of competence in your position in order to be assertive in this situation.

You will need to know how to stimulate trust, when and how to share information, and you need to become an expert listener. These types of managers develop strong teams and healthy organizational cultures. They understand the power of well thought out, consistent, and clearly articulated vision. They can quickly diagnose whether the team/organization is performing at full potential, delivering on commitments, and whether the team is changing and growing versus just operating.

As a manager, you may not be aware of how intimidating you might seem to your employees. Just saying, "My door is always open," will make you feel better, but it won't inspire your employees to take you up on it. The truth is "Open Door" policies just don't work. The best leaders, the leaders that people want to follow, are initiators. They leave their office and visit with their employees one on one or in groups. They don't just ask, "How's the project going?" They ask, "How are YOU doing?" and then really listen to the answer. Now, not all of you are naturally relational leaders, and you all have a lot on your plates. But great leaders that others want to follow will schedule time to intentionally care and connect with their team.

When this type of manager engages with their employees they will use those opportunities to seek feedback. They will not only ask, "How are you doing?" They ask, "How am I doing?" and "How are WE doing as a team?" If you want to be a leader that people want to follow, take time to sit down with your employees, both individually and as a team, and ask them to evaluate how you are doing as a leader.

Are you giving them what they need?

Do you have any blind spots that need to be addressed?

What are you doing that is helping them be successful?

What are you doing that might be getting in the way of them being successful?

How are we doing as a team?

Are the goals you've set for the year realistic?

Do they have what they need to achieve those goals?

How's morale? What can you do to improve?

Of course, you'll want to weigh the feedback you receive and run it past your key circle of advisors to get some clarity. It's a scary proposition because you may actually hear the truth, and the truth might hurt. But it will make you a better leader. It will also make your people want to run the distance with you because you've shown humility and respect for them.

To be assertive as a manager requires boundless energy. Great managers have a boundless amount of energy. They are positive in their outlook, and their attitude is contagious. A low energy leader is not motivating, convincing, or credible. Consequently, the energetic type of manager will never quit. They just simply refuse to lose. They have an insatiable appetite for accomplishment and results. While they may reengineer or change direction, they will never lose sight of the primary motivation / purpose of the organization.

A practical skill to help you be more assertive is to be the manager who celebrates success and respects failure. Do not ignore these events. A passive manager is not an assertive manager. You will not be able to effectively lead your team without being proactive in celebrating success and respecting failure. What do you do when your employees accomplishes something great? Or when one of your employees does something exceptional that reflects the organisation's core values? Do you celebrate it?

It might be as simple as a quick email that says you noticed and appreciate them. It might be something you talk about at a staff meeting or a team gathering. It might be a gift card for a lunch or coffee. Success needs to be celebrated! Perhaps even more important than how you celebrate success is how you show honor and respect when someone on your team tries something great that fails. Be interested in how a person talks about their failures than in what they have accomplished.

What did they learn from it?

How did it change them or cause them to grow?

What do they do differently now?

If you want to be a leader that people want to follow, celebrate the successes of your team but also honor and respect failure. Rather than simply chastising your employee for something that didn't work, use it as a teachable moment. Sit down with them and talk about what went wrong.

What can you learn from it?

What are ways that it can be redeemed?

The last key skill to learn in order to become more assertive and therefore more effective as a leader is to learn how to invest in your employee's futures, even if it means they may leave your team one day. Don't fret on the sidelines watching great employees come and go from your organisation – become proactive and assertive! Become active in their development and demonstrate that there is value in having them connect well with you. Help your employees recognize that you would be a great asset in their own personal growth.

You need to want the best for your employees. You need to invest time, energy, and other resources into helping your employees reach their potential as leaders in their own right. Be assertive here – take advantage of the opportunity that every one of your employees are giving you. They want to be successful and they are looking to you to help them do so. When you look at your employees always ask the question:

What is their next area of growth?

What would help them get there?

What can you as a leader, or you as an organization, provide for them to help them realize their potential?

Do you need to get them more training?

Do they need to be mentored?

Do they need more opportunities to try some things outside of their current role?

That investment may ultimately lead to a team member leaving to join another organisation, but it won't be because they don't want to follow your leadership. It will be because you prepared them to serve in new ways.

Celebration

10 Rules to an Effective Staff Meeting

Rule number one: Feed the staff

- The employee will be able to focus longer if they have food in their stomachs.
- The employee will be less likely to be distracted if they have food in their stomachs.
- Feeding them is also used as a morale boost.
- Having food can also work toward establishing a family team atmosphere.
- Think about having your staff bring a potluck breakfast or dinner one time as a fun thing to do.

Rule number two: Make it casual

- By reducing the general formalities around staff meetings, you can invite a more collaborative environment with your employees.
- Avoid running your meetings like a board meeting, using Robert's Rules of Order.
- You can have a general outline to the meeting but be prepared to adapt to the presenting needs of your employees.
- Consider your environment and set-up as the atmosphere contributes to the formality of the meeting.

Rule number three: Make it fast paced

- Keep the pace moving. If there are not a lot of questions to answer, do not wait for any to be asked.

- By keeping a quick pace, it will help the employee grasp concepts better. Keep in mind your environment. There is television which is entertainment divided into 10-second sound bites. There are movies, music and videos, that are very high paced. All of these factors stimulate your employees and if you cannot compete at least on some level, you run the risk of losing their interest.

Rule number four: Make it as short as possible

- Nobody likes a long staff meeting. If it is going to be an hour long, make sure that it is a packed hour.
- If it is going to be more than an hour long then make sure that it is as full as possible with an opportunity for a break of sorts half way through.
- Try to use a break as an opportunity to conduct a communication exercise or other interactive workshop as an example.

Rule number five: Pace yourself

- Make sure that you are spending as much time as is needed on each topic.
- Staying too long on any one topic is sure to have your employees tuning out for the remainder of the meeting.
- Do not stop to focus on distractions offered by employees.
- Discipline yourself to stay on schedule and avoid the pitfalls that employees may do to get you focused on their agendas.

Rule number six: Have an awards and/or recognition time

- Although this might seem difficult at first, the positive effects far outweigh any extra effort on your part. Individual recognition especially in a group setting is ideal for increasing the self-esteem of that person.

- You do not want to outdo yourself though and run the risk of your staff not appreciating the awards anymore.
- Use this opportunity to hand out an employee of the month award or simply sharing encouraging words about one of your employees. Recognizing beyond the call of duty items of specific employees could be another way to ensure that there will always be someone being recognized.

Rule number seven: Never conduct individual discipline

- A staff meeting is not the time to address corrective behavior of a single person.
- Do not issue verbal warnings or any type of progressive discipline at a staff meeting.
- Do not express your frustration or utter threats of future discipline at a staff meeting.
- If, during a staff meeting you have an employee who is trying to distract you or get you off topic do not make an example out of them and move on.
- A better approach would be to address the person with something like; "You seem to want to talk about something that is bothering you. After the staff meeting I will make myself available to talk to you if you would like but right now I need to complete the meeting." This will let the person know that their behavior is inappropriate but it still gives them an opportunity to settle any issues with you quickly and efficiently and in a private way.

Rule number eight: Explain the reasons for change

- If you are changing a policy, procedure, system or introducing a new one then make sure that you explain fully to your staff all of the reasons for the changes. "Just because", does not go over to well with our employees and they deserve to know why.

- Sometimes you are expected to introduce a policy or procedure that did not originate with yourself. If you do not know then make sure you find out before the staff meeting.
- Explaining why there are changes will help your staff accept them easier and therefore make your job easier in implementing them.

Rule number nine: Summarize

- Make sure that as you complete one section of your meeting and even at the end of the meeting that you leave some time for you to summarize all of the issues discussed.
- Review the key points, if necessary, before moving on.
- This will help ensure that you have not missed anything or an employee has not missed anything and it makes for a great transition into rule number ten.

Rule number ten: Questions and answers

- Always make room for a Q&A time.
- This could be done after each item of your meeting or left to the end.
- I would suggest if you have more than three items to discuss that you leave room at the end of the meeting for any questions and not after each section as you may find that all of your time will be consumed by the questions.

Oh Oh! My Employee Did Something Good. Now What?

Sometimes a praiseworthy event may go unnoticed or ignored by you, and this is not always a bad thing. Here are some points to consider:

A manager's job is to model appropriate behavior and to set / maintain the standard of performance. Therefore, the expectation is that the employee is accomplishing the objectives and expected outcomes of their position. These are not things to be praised necessarily but expected. Remember that you can only expect your employee to do as good a job as yourself.

The rule of thumb is that the lowest common denominator establishes itself as the new expected standard of performance. Thus, it is easy to have the entire department under perform and then when one employee reaches higher and accomplishes the pre-established standard, your tendency would be to offer praise to them. This is sending the wrong message.

Next is that you could confront the action or as I like to state, offer "fireworks praises". This 'off-the-cuff' approach to praising an employee is good in the small things but is seen as demoralizing if it remains the only method of recognition. This is a good place to start in terms of learning how to praise your employees but make sure it does not become your only way of praising your employees.

As a manager you need to develop a deliberate plan to celebrate successes. You need to be intentional in how you offer praise to your employees and you need to be consistent. Teamwork is built upon trust, good communication and high morale. Here are only a few ways to build morale for your team:

Celebration of personal events:

Celebrating the employee's birthday, work anniversary, milestones (such as graduation) are easy and inexpensive but very powerful in their effect. Something as simple as a birthday cake or even the gift of a company watch/clothing for graduation goes a long way toward letting your employees know how much they are appreciated. These types of celebration allow for the entire team to get involved thus building on that family atmosphere.

Personal recognition of personal events:

It is great feeling that an employee receives when they receive a card from their boss. It lets them know that they aren't a number but a person and that you appreciate them. Taking the time to write out a card to your employee no matter what the occasion will instill a sense of pride and accomplishment within your employee.

Group activities and events:

Holding a summer fun day or a potluck breakfast is just a couple of the fun activities that you can do. The key here is to create something that every employee is able to participate in and wants to participate in. This helps to gel the employees together into a family. Try asking your employees for ideas on some fun events that they may be interested in doing.

Delegation:

This will be either the favorite section of the manager or the most difficult. Delegation is a necessary part of your job but could be taken to the extreme. A good example is with the blue chips of the operation. These areas require your complete attention and cannot be delegated for extended periods of time. However, they can be taught to your employees and occasionally they can be assigned those tasks but in the overall picture you must remain in control of them.

To the manager that cannot delegate then may I say that the lack of delegation is a direct relationship to your lack of trust of your employees and this needs to be addressed. You may find yourself with many excuses as to why you do all the work instead of delegating but if you listen carefully to each of your reasons the underlining message will be one of distrust toward your employees. Take the time necessary to develop this skill, as it will prove most valuable to you and your team in the long run.

To the manager that wants to delegate everything to everyone around them may I suggest that perhaps you are reflecting your inability to manage / to lead. A manager needs to understand every aspect of their position intimately – which would be reflected in those blue chips that they control. If this is not the case then a self-assessment is necessary. If you would rather delegate everything then perhaps management is not the place for you to be.

Follow-up:

To start a project will require a commitment in order to finish it. To create an action plan for your team will require follow-up in order to complete it. Follow-up is your test of commitment to your issues that you have outlined to your team. When you mention a new program that you will be implementing but after a month there still is no new program there is a tendency for your team to start to lose respect for you as their manager.

It is likely that follow-up in some form or another is probably one of the key reasons to any manager's demise. Not following up adequately on inventory issues would be an example. Having a clear, measurable objective in the beginning will help you as the Manager complete the objective. You need to depend on your team to complete these objectives but it is your ability to follow-up that will ultimately determine its success.

Conclusion

Here you are at the end of this book. You have employed all of the strategies I have talked about with The Exit Strategy and you have developed an amazing team. However, make sure you understand how to keep those great employees. Here are some points to consider[xiii]:

First, you need to know that great employees hate stagnation. Great employees often exhibit certain common qualities: they have an appetite to learn, they master their jobs relatively quickly, they bore easily, and they are usually eager for the next challenge. If you can't provide them opportunities for growth, knowledge, and new experiences, they often will look elsewhere. A suggestion might be to involve such staff in meetings and projects where the deciding factor isn't how they contribute to the process or outcome, but rather how the process or outcome contributes to their professional development.

Make sure you have a strong, positive culture and a well-functioning organization with clear goals. This is really important to attract great employees, often by word of mouth from your existing employees. If you celebrate each employee's birthday and engage in activities that demonstrate that each person is valued and appreciated, employees can feel that they are part of something positive. People want to work in a positive atmosphere. If you make it a fun place to work, people are more likely to stay. Even more than good organizations, people work for good managers. The greatest managers are ones who keep the employee engaged, who trust that they know what they're doing, who encourage and offer constructive feedback.

Take note that no one enjoys working in a muddle. Establishing clear job descriptions, policies, objectives and metrics, and holding people accountable gives your employees the necessary tools to know when they are being successful. Employees feel particularly engaged when they clearly know how their work matters within the organization's strategic plan.

Remember that your employees have lives and dreams. The performance review or monthly coaching meeting is an incredible opportunity to engage your employees by using this time for two-way communication. This is an opportunity to find out what is important to your employees outside of work — and to discuss the potential for flexibility to allow them to engage in their personal passions and/or to attend to family responsibilities — as well as learning more about their career goals and how you can support them in their aspirations. This can result in work responsibilities still being achieved, while the employee feels motivated and appreciative for the ability to balance work/life. This can be very useful in terms of succession planning as well as helping employees use their strengths in their current roles.

One significant challenge for retaining great employees within most smaller organizations is the typical flat organizational structure that it offers. This flat structure means that, unlike larger organizations, there are fewer opportunities for promotion. However even within small organizations there are creative ways of expanding an employee's responsibilities and opportunities. Give these staff as many leadership responsibilities and opportunities as you can. Assign high performing staff to participate in or lead special projects or teams that is different from their day-to-day responsibilities.

Invest in opportunities for your employees to either be mentored by someone or to mentor someone themselves. Employees benefit from mentoring and learning from others. Keen employees want to keep learning and developing. In addition to offering learning opportunities and professional development, you need to be cultivating mentorship.

It may seem counterintuitive but one key way to keep great staff is to properly manage underperforming staff. Managers who do not manage poor performers, otherwise known as the toxic employee, will risk losing credibility among competent staff. Excusing or ignoring poor performance can be de-motivating to staff who successfully meet all objectives. Likewise, be sure to address any workplace conflicts as these can create stress for all staff, even those not directly involved.

It is important to understand that managers turned leaders are rare[xiv]. After studying 2.5 million work units over the last two decades, Gallup's research has shown that about 1 in 10 managers have the following traits to make them a leader. Unfortunately, not being a leader means you will end up with disenchanted employees and that process will always begin with the one you are interviewing.

A leader will engage the candidate with the culture, mission, and vision of your organization. Remember that the interview is not finding out if the person can do the job – that is useless. Instead find out if they fit with the culture. Find out if they have a passion for this work, for what you do. That is a leader finding a great employee.

A leader will be assertive. They will be intentional in all conversations with the employee. They will start the conversation and end the conversation. They will help keep the conversation on track. They will be accountable to the employee. They will be on time for all meetings with their employees. They will set clear timelines on when they will get back to the employee and they will expect the same from their employee. They will follow through with all commitments made to the employee.

A leader will establish a positive relationship with the employee from recruitment all the way through to termination. They will communicate worth and value to the employee. Remember; to be a successful leader you need to be successful as a person. To be successful as a person you need to start by looking truthfully into that mirror. You need to understand your limitations and prejudices, practice better communication, and foster healthy balanced relationships. Then, after everything is said and done place your trust in your abilities and your employee's abilities and that will create success for your employee.

At the end of the day the intent is that the shadow you cast will inspire your employees to strive after their own success. They begin their journey with you, mimicking your actions as they forge their own path. Then as you coach and develop them you are helping them toward success. Sometimes you will end up helping them find better places to fit in your organisation and sometimes you will end up helping them leave. But, at the end of the day you have communicated worth and value to each of your employees, you have demonstrated a commitment in their individual success and you have celebrated when they accomplished their goals. Their success becomes your success and that is the Exit Strategy.

THE EXIT STRATEGY

MICHAEL TOWERS, MA

[i] Material adapted from: http://www.inc.com/laura-entis/employee-engagement-is-costing-you.html?goback=%2Egde_1910740_member_205092536
[ii] Material adapted from: http://www.linkedin.com/today/post/article/20130519183133-15454-what-is-the-purpose-of-an-interview
[iii] Material adapted from: Leadership ideas from Bill Hybels
[iv] Material adapted from: http://www.linkedin.com/today/post/article/20140426191009-128811924-managers-beware-what-toxic-jane-or-joe-can-do-to-your-team?trk=eml-ced-b-art-M-2-9103295745876374255&midToken=AQG2yU107ET3eg&fromEmail=fromEmail&ut=2dKV-PveOyJ6c1
[v] Material adapted from: David Allen
[vi] Material adapted from: http://unews.utah.edu/news_releases/frequent-mulitaskers-are-bad-at-it/
[vii] Material adapted from: Tony Schwartz Wednesday March 14, 2012
[viii] Material adapted from: David Allen
[ix] Material adapted from: http://www.linkedin.com/today/post/article/20130520005409-36052017-are-you-making-this-mistake-at-the-end-of-your-meetings
[x] Material adapted from: http://www.xomba.com/confrontation
[xi] Material adapted from: http://www.constructiveconfrontation.com/top10myths/index.php)
[xii] Material adapted from: http://www.bigisthenewsmall.com/2013/12/20/15-traits-of-great-leadership/15 Traits Of Great Leadership
[xiii] Material adapted from: https://charityvillage.com/Content.aspx?topic=Worth_their_weight_in_gold_Ten_secrets_for_keeping_your_star_employees
[xiv] Material adapted from: http://blogs.hbr.org/2014/03/why-good-managers-are-so-rare/

REFERENCES

www.ingramcontent.com/pod-product-compliance
Lightning Source LLC
Chambersburg PA
CBHW052256220526
45471CB00001B/355